Finding
Your
Fairy Tale
Ending

Dechari Cole

Finding Your Fairy Tale Ending

B&H
PUBLISHING GROUP
Nashville, Tennessee

978-1-4336-8125-7

Published by B&H Publishing Group
Nashville, Tennessee

Dewey Decimal Classification: 248.83
Subject Heading: HAPPINESS \ GIRLS \ VIRTUE

1 2 3 4 5 6 7 8 • 17 16 15 14 13

To God—Thank You for writing the greatest love story ever told, and thank You that I get to be a part of it. I continue to be amazed by Your love.

And to the girls reading this book—I pray that you find your true identity, and discover that there is an amazing journey that awaits you when you seek God with all your heart.

—Dechari

Contents

Preface

Searching for Your Fairy Tale Ending

Fairy tales paint such wonderful pictures of love. While they always start with the search and struggle to find love, we take comfort in knowing that the ending will be amazing. We watch and read these stories of romance and happiness, and we so long for that to be us. *When will my prince charming come? When will I find my happy ending?* It's true that we all search for love—in different ways, in different people, in different things. But somewhere along the way, we begin to think that fairy tales are only stories—stories too perfect to be true. But are they?

I'm going to go ahead and let you in on a little secret: you can have a fairy tale ending. You can have joy and true love that surpasses even what you see in the movies . . . it just might not be exactly what you had planned or even dreamed of.

My own search for love started in high school. As a girl, I wanted someone who would make me feel special, loved, and cared for. That desire led to several dating relationships . . . and lots of valuable lessons! But as I searched for happiness in dating, I found happiness in other things, as well. For me, high school was a time to grow, experience life, learn more about who God is, and create friendships that would last a lifetime. God was writing my story—and high school was a big part of it.

Through God's blessing, I am going to share with you my story of love, friendship, and finding true fulfillment. So join me as I relive my high school and college years—both the good and the bad—in my search for love and my fairy tale ending. As I give you glimpses into my life, I'll let you know what I learned from my experiences and give you time to reflect on your own life. The "Girl Talk" sections will give you questions to think about and discuss—and they're great for doing together with your girlfriends. Along the way, I hope to encourage you to live a life of purity and faith and to let your light shine brightly in this world. My prayer is that you will live a life full of joy, and—as you realize all that God offers—you will see that His perfect plan is well worth the wait!

And the story begins . . .

All of my family was there—brothers, sister, nieces, nephews, mom, dad, in-laws, and in-laws-to-be, along with our closest friends. They had all arrived to witness this most special of days.

Everything was ready. Candelabras were draped with ivy and cascading white roses. Bouquets of more white roses were laid out for my attendants. An archway glittered with lights for our guests to pass through as they entered, mirroring the one on the stage where this new beginning would take place. The guest book was open, and white wicker baskets held programs that read, "Once upon a time . . ."

In the dressing room, my three best friends and my sister were already clothed in lovely, deep lilac dresses that flowed to the floor. When it was time to put on my own dress, I raised my arms as they lifted the gown above my head. They laced me up with a satin ribbon and fluffed the dress which spilled out in rich folds of white, dancing with silver and rhinestone accents and filling almost half the room. From underneath my hair, a satin-edged veil of white flowed down my back. On my head, I wore a small tiara—the perfect accent for my dress. When I slipped on my shoes with their twinkling rhinestones, I truly felt like a princess.

But even though everything and everyone looked so lovely, and so many details and so much work had been done, none of that really mattered. What truly mattered was that on this day I would marry my best friend—the man I have grown to care for more than any other on this earth, the one I have so much fun with, the one who can always make me smile, the one with whom I can truly be myself, and the one who was given to me (and I to him) as a great blessing from God. This was the day that my fairy tale would come true, and I would marry my prince charming.

I know it sounds as if I am giving away the fairy tale ending without giving you the rest of the story. And, believe me, it was a journey—there were lots of frogs before finding my prince! Every girl dreams of finding her own prince charming, but how do you find him, and how do you really know that he is *the one*? Well, God works in mysterious ways, and He brings people and things into our lives that we would sometimes never expect. Over time, He has opened my eyes to see how my path not only brought me closer to *finding* the right one, but also to *becoming* the right one. As I go back and tell you my story leading up to this fairy tale day, I hope you learn to trust that God will lead you to a great ending, too—as long as you let Him be your guide all along the way.

A man's heart plans his way,
but the LORD determines his steps.
(Proverbs 16:9)

Chapter 1

The Foundation:
It All Starts Here

Every story has it's beginning, and this is mine.

Everyone has a story to tell. Some are happy, exciting, joyful, and funny. Others are sad, scary, terrifying, and serious. But most of the time, I find that true stories include all of these elements. That's because a story isn't just about a moment; it's about a journey. And a journey is typically a search for something—even though the character may not realize at first what she is actually searching for.

Now, my most favorite stories always begin with *"Once upon a time. . . ."*

"Wait a minute!" you might say. "Your story doesn't actually have a prince, a princess, a king, a castle, frogs, an evil force, true love, and a fairy tale ending, does it?"

Well, yes, actually it does. Okay, maybe not the castle, but definitely all the rest. My journey, like many others, started with a search for love. And like all the best stories, it had lots of ups and downs, twists and turns, and—best of all—a surprise ending.

At the time, though, I didn't *know* that my life's story was being written or even that anything spectacular or worth talking about would come from it. You see, I was just the girl next door. I didn't have super talents, super parents, or come from a super place. I was just . . . well . . . ordinary. So before we dive into the journey to my fairy tale ending, let me tell you about where it all began—the foundation of the story, you might say.

My story starts in a tiny town in North Carolina, on twenty-three acres of land that sat pretty much in the middle of nowhere. I had two older brothers and a younger sister. We had goats, rabbits, horses, a pit bull, and a garden. It wasn't quite a farm, but it was pretty close. Our town consisted of one elementary school, one gas station that doubled as a grocery, one community swimming pool, and the Dairy Shack, where we got the best banana splits around. No, there wasn't even one single stoplight! I spent my days picking cherries, climbing trees, and riding my bike. Yep, a pretty normal little country girl.

Our family didn't have much money, so we didn't go or do a lot. But we did take one special trip each summer—and that was to the beach. On one of those trips, when I was six, I decided to go out to the big waves with my older brothers (who were seven and thirteen years older than me, I should point out). Now, I'm not sure what kind of beach you're used to, but Carolina waves can be quite large at times and the undercurrents are pretty strong.

One of my brothers thought it would be safe to pull me out in his new inflatable boat. Unfortunately, the waves were so rough that the boat flipped completely over and I went under. I quickly tried to stand, but the waves crashed relentlessly down on me, while the undercurrent churned me into the sand. I finally made it up and out of the ocean, but I couldn't see! The salt and sand had covered my eyes, burning them horribly. I panicked and started blindly running—but away from my family! That is, until a hand grabbed my arm and said, "Stop running. I've got you." It was my dad. He cleaned me up and told me I would be okay. "Oh, but the sand, the churning! It was awful!" I said, trying to explain how terrible it was not to be able to stand and get my head above water.

For the rest of the day, I only stood near the ocean's edge as the waves gently washed over my feet and the pull of the tide slowly took the sand out from under me. I remember being fascinated by how easily the waves shifted the sand. Later, about an hour before sundown, my dad took us to another part of the beach where a wall of rocks stood out in the water. He told us about his childhood adventures of walking the rocks way out into the ocean, to an island that we could barely see in the distance. Together, we walked quite a ways out, though we didn't have time to make it all the way to the island. I was *definitely* farther out than I had been when I went under earlier, but this time, I was standing on rock. The rocks allowed me to stand above the waves; they didn't shift like the sand.

Not too long after my experience with the rough ocean waves, I was hit with some rough waves in life. For though our beach trips were fun, and our simple life seemed good, my parents struggled in their marriage. My dad became verbally abusive to my mom. One night, the yelling was so bad that one of my brothers came into my room and said that if anything bad ever happened, I should go to the doghouse and Spike would protect me until he got there. Thankfully, it never came to that, but my life did take a rough turn.

One day after school, when I was supposed to go to piano lessons, my mom's friend picked me up and said there had been a change of plans. When I asked her why, she just said, "Everything's going to be okay." When I heard those words, I instantly knew something was very wrong. As we pulled up to our house, I saw my mom and sister already outside with our luggage packed. The car was quickly loaded, and we took off. No one would tell me where we were going. All I kept hearing was, "Everything is going to be okay." But I wasn't quite so sure.

After driving for a while, we ended up at a big, white house. "This is where we're going to stay for a while," my mom told me. It was a home for battered and abused women. I was only eight years old, and my whole world had just been turned upside down in an instant. My family, my house, my

For all have sinned and fall short of the glory of God.
—Romans 3:23

school, my friends had all suddenly slid out from beneath my feet. But still, I was able to stand.

You see, about a year before this took place, I had something big happen in my life. Though my family wasn't perfect (no one is—check out Romans 3:23), we went to church just about every time the doors were open. For years, I had heard about Jesus, God's Son. I heard about how He died on the cross to pay for my sins and that He was the only way to become right with God again. One night, I felt a desire in my heart to know Jesus personally and to live for Him. So I prayed and asked God to forgive my sins. I confessed that I believed in what Jesus did, and I asked Jesus to come and live in me with His Holy Spirit . . . and a relationship was born. Even though I was young, I had such an amazing friendship with Jesus. I knew He cared about me—yes, little ole me, in the middle of nowhere, with nothing super special. So when the waves of my parents' separation came crashing down on me, I was able to stand because Jesus was—and still is—my rock (Psalm 62:6).

In Matthew 7:24–27, Jesus talks about two men: one who built his house on the sand and one who built his house on rock. The man who built his house on the sand had a shaky foundation. The house looked nice, but it wasn't built on anything strong or reliable. When the storms came, the sand shifted and the house fell. But the house that had been built on the rock was able to withstand the storms because its foundation was strong.

> He alone is my rock and my salvation, my stronghold; I will not be shaken.
> —Psalm 62:6

This story reminds me of my beach experience. When I tried to stand on the sand, the waves pulled it right out from under me. But when I stood on the rocks, the waves didn't affect me. What Jesus was teaching in His example is that God's Word is the only strong foundation we can build our lives on. Everything else can be pulled out from under our feet. Life is imperfect, people will let us down, and the world will misguide us, but God and His

Word will never waver or lead us wrong. Because I had put my faith in Jesus, when I wasn't able to be strong, He was strong for me. My parents' separation was an opportune time for me to freak out and take off running in a direction that I shouldn't. But my heavenly Father grabbed my arm and said, "It's okay. I've got you." And I knew He did. Every story has its sad moments and its struggles, but like Paul says in Romans 8:28, "We know that all things work together for the good of those who love God: those who are called according to His purpose."

And God *did* bring good out of that terrible time. He took the most painful event in our family and used it to bring us closer to Him. Though I never got to move back home and my parents' divorce finalized, God still gave me joy as a young girl. He even provided a teacher's helper that first year at my new school who was a Christian and encouraged me daily.

My parents' walk with God became different too. My dad began to see the good in the things around him, and he became happier than I had ever seen him. He loves looking at God's beauty in nature and reads his Bible often. My mom grew in her confidence and her faith. Her struggles have allowed her to reach out to others who are hurting and give them hope. Because of her strong belief in prayer, she is called upon daily by her church, family, and friends to pray for God's help and guidance. My oldest brother decided to give his life to Jesus during an overnight stay in prison when he was being rebellious. Then, to his surprise, God called him to preach, and he has been pastoring a church alongside his wife and four wonderful children. My other brother, who was always trying to protect me, is now protecting our country by serving in the military. He is married and has three great kids. He shares his faith with those who have the hard lives of being in the military. My younger sister has always been amazing with kids. God allowed her and her husband to adopt two children who were in need of a good home, and they then had two children of their own. It's wonderful to see how she pours so much into her children and teaches them about God's love.

As for me, well, my story has been interesting—and I'm about to take you along on that journey. But I first wanted you to see the foundation of my story, because everything in my life builds off my relationship with Jesus and my belief in the truth of God's Word. Just as Jesus talked about in Matthew 7, your foundation can be something that is shifting and unstable like the sand—things like friends, popularity, sports, or school. These things can be tossed about with the waves and storms, destroying whatever is standing on them. Or you can build your life on the Rock—and I can say that building my life on the rock of God has allowed me to stand strong above the waves and to go farther out into the ocean than I would've ever dared on my own.

With Jesus as my Rock, I made it through those early tidal waves. Little did I know, though, that the waves coming at me in the distance were even bigger. There was a storm coming, and it was called high school. There my foundation in God would be tested like never before. Would I really follow God's leading and stand strong above the waves when my peers were telling me just to go with the flow—like sand tossed by the ocean waves? Would I still listen to God's instructions for how to live my life with the thunder booms of society shouting for me to settle for doing it their way? Well, I was out to find that treasure of true love, and I believed that following God's Word was the path that would lead me there. So are you ready to take this journey with me? Ok, here we go . . .

Once upon a time . . .

What I Learned

Though beachfront property may look good, don't be a fool by putting your faith in a foundation that isn't solid. Instead, build on the foundation of God's Word—it will stand the test of time.

My salvation and glory depend on God, my strong rock. My refuge is in God. Trust in Him at all times, you people; pour out your hearts before Him. God is our refuge. (Psalm 62:7–8)

Girl Talk '

1. Jesus says that God's Word is our only true foundation for life, and Matthew 7 actually talks a lot about how we should live. Read all of Matthew 7 for yourself. What foundation principles for your life can you find?

_____

_____

_____

_____

2. I made it through my parents' divorce by leaning on Jesus' strength. When something tough comes crashing down on you, where do you run for strength? Have you ever run from God? Sometimes it seems that when you need someone the most, no one is around. Might that be because God wants you to run to Him?

_____

_____

_____

_____

3. Can you think of an experience in your life that seemed negative at first, but that later turned out for good? Did you become stronger for it? Can you think of any biblical examples of this?

_____

_____

_____

_____

4. Do you think your trials can be used to bring glory to God and to point others to Him? How can your struggles affect your relationship with God?

_____

_____

_____

_____

5. If you aren't the one going through an immediate crisis, do you know someone who is? Can you lift him or her up in prayer? What other ways can you be supportive? Be specific!

_____

_____

_____

_____

6. Now that you know the foundation for my story, what's yours?

_____

_____

_____

_____

Chapter 2

High School . . .
and the Dating Begins

Decide what your boundaries are—and then stick to them!

❧❧❧❧❧❧❧❧❧❧❧❧

The summer before my freshman year, I took Driver's Ed up at the high school—which was a sure sign that I was growing up. (I also made the wise choice to let my perm grow out that summer, so that I looked like a normal person again!) I was leaving my childhood days behind and getting ready for a new adventure in life.

It was really exciting for me when high school finally started. I had a little more freedom, and I enjoyed getting to pick some of my classes. I was meeting new people, as well as becoming even closer to old friends. Of course, it didn't take long for my attention to turn to the new guys I was seeing around school. Although, I'd had some "boyfriends" when I was younger, that consisted of . . . well . . . not really anything except having the title of boyfriend and girlfriend. Suddenly, I had guys asking me out to the movies, out to eat, and just to hang out. I was moving up

That Little Voice: Learning to Listen to the Holy Spirit

- Your initial gut feeling is usually right. That hesitation may be the Holy Spirit whispering to you.

- When faced with a decision, ask yourself how it compares to God's Word. For example, God wouldn't want you to be too intimate with your boyfriend because He says you should flee sexual immorality (1 Corinthians 6:18).

- If you're hiding something, then it's probably wrong. God wants you to be a light in this world, not hide your actions in the darkness.

- Work at pleasing God instead of your peers. Continually pray for His guidance, and then listen and watch for Him to show you what to do.

in the world, and I didn't mind being a little fish in a big pond. I was ready to swim!

About a week or two after school started, a freshman guy approached me in the hall. He had blond hair, blue eyes, and was really cute! He asked if I would like to come to a party he was having. I remember thinking that this was probably not the kind of party I would feel good about going to. Don't get me wrong—I love to have fun. If people think Christians don't have fun, they are sorely mistaken. But I just didn't feel right about this party. Remember, God gives us the Holy Spirit to help us discern things. I kind of made a comment about how I didn't really "party." He said, "Okay," and went on to class.

I didn't realize it then, but I was already choosing the path I would take. By just saying no to that one person, I was saying no to a lifestyle and a group of friends that would not have been the best for me. Later, I heard that he did drugs and drank alcohol. And while he never asked me to another party, he was still nice to me. Just because you don't do things that others may do, doesn't always mean that they'll make fun of you. I didn't put him down, and he didn't put me down. We just believed in different things.

Since "party guy" wasn't on my list of potential dates, I continued to keep my eyes open. My friends introduced me to two guys in particular. Both were freshman, and both wanted to get to know me. And while both seemed nice, one was a little more outgoing and "cool." The other was a little more love-struck and slightly shy. I decided to date the "cool" guy. His name was Justin.

Justin and I were going to go to the movies for our first date. I really hadn't been on a date before, so I asked some mutual friends to come along. (I think this also helped my mom agree to the date!) Being in a group helped take a little of the pressure off. It also gave me a chance to see how he acted with his friends and mine. Unfortunately, we didn't stick to the group dates. We ended up going to the movies more often and hanging out at his house by ourselves. (Just so you know—this was *not* a good idea.)

Justin gave me my first kiss; I think it was on our second date. In a way, I was flattered, but I had just met this guy not that long ago. Why was I kissing him before I had true, deep feelings for him? At the time, I thought that was just part of having a relationship. However, it didn't take long for me to realize the temptations there are in having a relationship.

Since I had already chosen to stay pure, I knew that there were boundaries I would not cross. I think, though, that guys struggle with this type of temptation even more than girls. It was a long time before I truly realized how much of an effect a girl can have on a guy. I had always heard youth leaders say how girls need to be careful about the way we dress, so as not to be a temptation, but I had never thought much about it. I wasn't trying to be a temptation; I just dressed in what I thought was cute. Of course, as girls, we *do* like attention and for people to think we're pretty. But for guys, it can be a really big struggle to be around a girl in short shorts, for example, especially in a setting with no one else around.

I started feeling uncomfortable with Justin wanting to kiss as much as we did. It was the same feeling I had with "party guy." I knew it wasn't what I should be doing, and honestly I enjoyed our time doing activities together better. I finally told Justin that I wanted to take a step back, to just enjoy hanging out together and not kiss for a while. But it wasn't long before I realized that Justin didn't want to just hang out or get to know me better. He was looking for something more physical. When I stood up for my beliefs, he eventually cheated on me with another girl. You'd think I would have been angry and hurt, but honestly I counted it as a blessing and a big wake-up call. I had learned that there should be more to dating than just kissing. I wasn't going to give up on having a boyfriend—I just knew I needed a better one.

What I Learned

If all a boy wants to do is kiss you, he's not really interested in *you*.

≈≋≈

I say then, walk by the Spirit and you will not carry out the
desire of the flesh. (Galatians 5:16)

Girl Talk

1. Have you ever heard that little voice inside you whisper, "Don't do that"? That's God, trying to guide you away from harm. If I hadn't paid attention to His Spirit telling me to avoid the party scene, or that my relationship with Justin wasn't right, then my freshman year would have looked a lot different. You'll have to make lots of choices in life. Will you listen to God's voice? Or ignore it because you don't want to "miss out"?

_____

_____

_____

_____

2. Check out these verses about the Holy Spirit: Romans 8:26–27, Galatians 5:16–25, John 14:15–18, Acts 4:31, and 1 Corinthians 2:10–16. What do these verses tell you about the Holy Spirit leading you and how you can learn from Him? Can you find other verses?

_____

_____

_____

_____

3. Do you think things would have been different for Justin and me if we had stuck with the group dates and activities? Do you put yourself in situations where it would be easy to get physical with your boyfriend?

_____

_____

_____

_____

4. Do you know where you stand on being physical in a relationship? Set some boundaries for yourself, and write them down. It's much easier to stick to a decision you've already made.

_____

_____

_____

_____

5. We can't just blame guys for their struggles with intimacy. If we truly care about the guys around us, we should try to make their struggles easier instead of harder. How can you help protect the purity of the guys around you?

_____

_____

_____

_____

6. My friend's father once told her, "You have a choice: Do you want to be liked now or respected forever?" What's your answer? Will you go with the flow? Or stand up for what you believe?

_____

_____

_____

_____

Chapter 3

You Can Have Fun . . .
with God?

Good friends can keep you on the right path.

Well, since things didn't work out with Justin, I decided to focus on making friends and getting to know people—while still keeping an eye out for that special someone. Actually, the other guy I mentioned—the one I chose not to date—ended up becoming a good friend. His name was Jason. We had P.E. together, and it was there that we got to know each other better. He still wanted to date me, but I decided we made better friends.

One day, my friend Carol Ann and I ended up meeting some guys on the school bus, and they invited us to come to their church. Their youth group was getting ready to go on a mission trip of sorts to do some skits at a few churches and then go to an amusement park. That sounded fun. Even though Carol Ann and I both went to church, we weren't really involved in the youth groups. So, we visited their church one Wednesday night to see what it was all about and if we wanted to go on this Christian drama tour.

As Carol Ann and I walked into the church, this very outgoing—and slightly crazy—man ran over to say hello. He took my hand as if he were going to kiss it, but then kissed his own instead! It made me laugh, but also made me wonder, *Who is this guy?!* He later walked up on stage, and I realized *he* was the pastor!

As the evening got started, I was amazed. I had never seen a group of people this excited about being together and praising God. And also . . . *it was fun!* It wasn't at all solemn the way church had sometimes felt to me in the past. There was still awe and reverence for God, but there was also a great joy in their worship. Somehow I had been missing the fact that you can have fun with God.

Somehow I had been missing the fact that you can have fun with God.

After that first night, Carol Ann and I were hooked. I was learning to see the joy in my salvation and in what God was doing in my life—and I got to celebrate it every week with other believers. I invited Jason as well as another great friend, Kristy, and several others to come to the church and to go on the drama tour. Turns out, this was to be to the beginning of a great group of Christian friends.

Over the next few weeks and months, I learned how to praise God with a joyful heart. I looked forward to going to church—it refreshed me and helped me make it through the rest of the week. I also became really close to the people in youth group. At least ten of them went to my school and eight were in my freshman class. It was great to have friends who loved God and who were by my side at school. They held me accountable and helped keep me out of trouble and on a good path. Believe me, if I had done anything, one of them would have known! And besides, I was having fun—without having to get drunk, be promiscuous, or do drugs.

My friends and I went to youth rallies, where I first heard upbeat Christian music and speakers who talked about things that were important to us as teens. Jason and Kristy even got saved at one of those rallies! Then I thought, *What if Carol Ann or I had never invited them to church or the youth rallies?* I realized then how important it was to share my faith, so I started telling anyone I got close to at school about how much I loved church and inviting them to come too. I knew how awesome it was to live for God, and I wanted others to have that joy too.

After Jason got saved, we became even closer friends. He became someone I could count on to lift me up if I were feeling down. He always made me laugh—whether I wanted to or not. And Carol Ann was there as my best girlfriend, always ready to listen and give me godly advice. I could count on her for anything. I also had friends who knew a lot about the Bible, who could help me better understand it. Other friends had amazing talents—like singing and playing instruments—and they used those talents for God. These were the kind of friends that God was giving me. They helped me, and I hope I helped them.

In life, you really need a good support team. People who love you for who you are, and who will be there through your highs and lows, to give advice and prayer, to give an outside point of view, and to just live life together with. Friends can either lift you up or pull you down. So choose your close friends carefully, because they are a huge part of shaping the person you'll be in the future.

What I Learned

Nothing shapes you more than who and what you surround yourself with. So choose wisely—good friends will lift you up and push you toward God.

🌿

Iron sharpens iron, and one man sharpens another.
(Proverbs 27:17)

Girl Talk

1. Nehemiah 8:10 tells us that our strength is in the joy of the Lord. Spending time worshiping God and having good, clean fun with other Christians filled my spirit and got me through the week with joy. Have you learned to have fun with God? How so, or why not?

_____

_____

_____

_____

2. Are you surrounding yourself with good Christian friends? What can you do to build up a good support group who will sharpen you and bring you closer to God? How can you sharpen others in their faith?

_____

_____

_____

_____

3. It's important to have godly people for your closest friends, but you also need to share Jesus with others. How can you do both? Here's a tip: take a look at Jesus' life. He reached out to sinners, but He also spent a lot of time with His closest disciples. What might that look like in your life?

_____

_____

_____

_____

4. Are you inviting your non-Christian friends and classmates to church or telling them about God? If you don't, who will? TV? Magazines? Music? Definitely not! Pray that God will open up opportunities for you to share Him with others. It can be as easy as telling them

about the great things God has done for you, or how He has comforted you in hard times.

_____

_____

_____

_____

5. You share with your friends when you have good news, right? So why do you think people are so hesitant to share the Good News of Jesus? Why are you?

_____

_____

_____

_____

Chapter 4

Superficial

True love isn't just skin deep.

I was really blessed with the friendships I formed in high school, and I enjoyed the time I spent with those friends. But I still found myself looking for that one guy who would make me feel special. As I kept my eyes open for that special someone, one guy caught my eye. He was a friend of my friend Josh. Josh and I had gone to elementary school together and were fairly close. *So,* I thought, *a guy who's cute and a friend of someone I know. This could be good.* I decided to make the extra effort to talk to Josh when this guy was around.

Everything worked as planned, and Josh introduced me to Brad. I'm sure that my flirty eyes and smile gave away the fact that I thought Brad was cute. Though I wasn't sure at the time what impression I had made, Josh told me later that Brad thought I was really pretty. *Cool!* Two people with a mutual attraction can't be a bad start, right? Josh passed on the initial messages between Brad and me, that we were interested in each other. I know, a little elementary school, but who cares? I got the guy.

Brad and I decided to go to the school's upcoming dance together. The dance was close to Valentine's Day, and I expected it to be so romantic. It was also my first real dance. I spent hours doing my hair and makeup, only to keep going back to the mirror to make sure I still looked okay.

Brad came to the door to pick me up, and my mom grabbed the camera. Even my little sister pulled me aside to say how cute she thought Brad was. After the pictures, Brad's parents drove us to the school and dropped us off. We spent the first hour socializing with other friends and getting more pictures taken. So far it was a lot of fun . . . then came the time to actually dance!

I was a little intimidated at first as Brad and I made our way out on the dance floor. My heart was racing as I stepped close to him and started to raise my arms above his shoulders. *But wait! Do I put my hands on top of his shoulders or drape them over his back? Do I touch his neck? Interlock my fingers? Where should my hands go?!* I could tell he was probably thinking the same thing about his hands. Well, wherever our hands landed, we did start to dance, swaying as our feet lightly lifted right then left. Brad was so cute, and being so close made my blood pressure rise. I did try once or twice to look him in the eye, but—*whoa!*—that was uncomfortable. Less eye contact was *definitely* easier. After swaying a while, we actually started to move in a small circle. Yeah, maybe not the most romantic, sweep-you-off-your-feet dance of all time, but still pretty wonderful.

After the dance, we went back to Brad's house with some friends to watch a movie. I sat next to Brad, of course. We smiled at each other now and then, but it seemed like we had more to say to other people than to each other. It wasn't that I didn't want to talk to Brad, but I couldn't seem to carry on a good conversation with him. Once the movie started, it relieved the pressure of having to talk very much. The night ended with Brad's parents driving me home and him walking me to the door. I don't remember exactly how he said goodnight, but I do know his parents were watching. So if I got a kiss, it was most definitely the quickest peck you've ever seen.

After the dance, when Valentine's Day actually came around, Brad and I were supposed to get each other something. But what do you get for a cute guy you've just started seeing? I was clueless. I couldn't get a guy a stuffed animal, and the heart-shaped box of chocolates didn't seem right either. Where were the "I think you're cute" presents? In the end, I made my own set of chocolates that said "I [[heart symbol]] U." It was so awkward! All I remember is Josh standing across the hall, telling Brad that I tried.

Shortly after Valentine's Day had passed (thank goodness), I would see Brad here and there between classes, hanging out and laughing with his friends. He played hackie sack with them a lot and talked about different outdoor activities, like rock climbing. That was the stuff that Brad was all about. I started to realize that we didn't have much in common or much to talk about. And we *definitely* didn't laugh and have fun like he did with his friends—or like I did with mine. That initial attraction was still there, but it didn't seem to matter so much anymore. Having a cute boyfriend was no longer enough, and I began to see that this relationship was only skin deep. It was . . . *superficial.*

Having a cute boyfriend was no longer enough.

It didn't take long for us both to realize the same thing. I don't even remember how the relationship officially ended—it was that smooth of a break-up. Most likely Josh relayed those messages too! Brad was a good guy, but he just wasn't the guy for me. Because of the way our relationship had been, though, it was easy to transition to just being friends. We had no hard feelings, no broken hearts, and no regrets. Honestly, a big part of that was because we were never physical in our relationship. We were never even in a position to kiss, because we were always hanging out at school or with groups of people. And you know . . . it was really nice that way.

I never regretted dating Brad. It actually helped me realize more about what I needed in a relationship. I needed someone I could have fun with and relate to. And I needed something deeper than that initial, superficial attraction, because a crush is short-lived.

I also began to understand why so many relationships come to an abrupt end. I think people often do what I did—look only at the outward things like a person's appearance, how they dress, money, physical attraction, their influence, or social status. Take, for example, the cutest guy in your school. There's always at least one who stands out as drop-dead gorgeous. He's usually an athlete of some sort who looks great and dresses well. Everyone wants to be his friend. Well, what if that guy asked you out? Your heart would race, your face would flush, and you would totally say yes, right? It's just human nature, but it's also superficial if that's all you have. Relationships based on superficial things will be short-lived.

I was glad that I didn't let my crush on Brad go on too long. Thankfully, we realized our differences early on. By hanging out in our normal surroundings of friends and school, it was easier to see that we weren't compatible. I think if Brad and I had been more physical, then we probably would have stayed together longer—but for the wrong reasons. I know it would have made the break-up so much harder when those romantic feelings faded and we found there was nothing more. Instead, I was thankful that we got to know each other the way we did. I was able to easily go on with my life, unhurt, and continue my search for the perfect guy.

What I Learned

While appearances can be pleasing to the eye, beauty alone gets boring after a while.

Charm is deceptive and beauty is fleeting, but a woman who fears the LORD will be praised. (Proverbs 31:30)

Girl Talk

1. If you are currently in a relationship, what is keeping you in it? Is it just physical attraction? The attention? How can you make sure it's not superficial?

_____

_____

_____

_____

2. What's a healthy approach for getting to know someone, so that if it doesn't work out you're not left with a broken heart or regrets?

_____

_____

_____

_____

3. Not speaking just romantically, but in general, do you feel that you give people a chance? Do you try to get to know them no matter what their appearance is? Are there people who have surprised you once you got to know them—both good and bad?

_____

_____

_____

_____

4. Are you more than your appearance? Of course, you are! So what are you doing to work on your inward beauty as well as your outward beauty?

_____

_____

_____

_____

Chapter 5

Learning to Steer on My Own

With freedom comes responsibility.

❧❧❧❧❧❧❧❧❧❧❧❧

Well, Justin and Brad took up most of my freshman year. Soon, I was a sophomore and no longer the new kid on the block. I was still active in church and close to my same group of friends, but this year I would get to know a whole new group of friends. This was the year I would broaden my horizons and get to know a group of juniors. And that was definitely going to change things.

My P.E. coach that year was also the head of Fellowship of Christian Athletes (FCA). One day, he mentioned to me that several students got together in the mornings before school to have a short Bible study and to pray. Carol Ann, Kristy, and I decided to give it a try, and we ended up going pretty much every day. Talking about God and praying with our classmates became a really nice way to start the day—and helped make the not-so-great days a little more bearable. A few different students took turns leading the lesson, but there was one guy who did it most of the time. He was a junior named Chris.

I got to know Chris as a friend and would often say hi in the halls. This, of course, gave me the opportunity to meet some of his other junior friends. And just so you know, even though I probably had boys on my mind half of the time, this was not the reason I was saying hi to Chris. However, I couldn't help but notice that Chris had several cute friends. They were a fun, outgoing crowd, and I enjoyed hanging out with them between classes. They ended up calling me by my last name, "Moose"—a nickname that stuck throughout high school. I didn't mind, though; it was their way of saying I was part of the group. And it was kind of funny. "Moose" makes you picture some big football player, but no, it was just little ole me.

As I got to know this group of guys, I found out that practically all of them worked at the grocery store about a quarter of a mile from my house. My mom and I talked about how it could be a good thing if I got a part-time job there too. I was sixteen, but without a car. Since the store was within walking distance, though, it was no big deal. Plus, the extra shopping money sounded great, *and* I would be working with friends. I applied and was hired. I had my first job!

So now I was working for a living in addition to going to school. Okay, maybe I wasn't working for a *living*, but I was working. With my new job, I had more responsibilities, and it was a great time to grow and decide what kind of person I was going to be. Of course, that's not exactly what I was thinking at the time. My thinking was more along the lines of "I like paychecks!" Nevertheless, I did think about what kind of employee I wanted to be. It had always frustrated me in the past when I saw employees who acted as if they hated being at work. I decided to be the opposite. As a cashier, I tried to be extra friendly to the customers and let them know I was happy to see them. It made my customers happy and made my job more enjoyable too. I leaned on God every day to help me, because He knew there were some days I didn't feel like smiling.

So . . . good attitude? *Check*. Now on to the being responsible part. I had to make sure I wasn't late for work. With my friends, I was known for being fashionably ten minutes late, but that wouldn't cut it in the work world. I needed to plan my time so that didn't happen, as well as juggle time between friends, church, and homework. As I ran from one thing to another, my mom allowed me to become more and more responsible for myself, my actions, and my time. I was steering my own life in a lot of ways now . . . well . . . minus the actual car.

I continued to work hard and have a good attitude toward the customers and other employees. Soon, the store manager took notice. He asked me what I thought about working in the office, helping him and the assistance manager count the money drawers. I was a little shocked, but also honored. The office was where all the money and important papers were kept, and regular employees weren't allowed up there. I knew that this meant he trusted me.

I was learning that trust is a big thing—not only at work, but in all of my relationships. It was important for my mom to trust me; otherwise, she wouldn't let me go and do as much as I did. It was important that my friends trust me, or else they wouldn't feel safe sharing their lives and troubles with me. I began to see that trust is key to having meaningful relationships. I wanted to be someone people could count on, and I knew that I wanted that in my future husband too. I wanted someone who would be faithful, who would keep God in our relationship, and who would lift me up, not pull me down. Ultimately, I wanted a guy I could trust with my heart. I hadn't found him yet, but I hoped to one day.

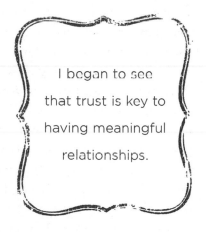

I began to see that trust is key to having meaningful relationships.

Because I helped close the store several nights a week, I ended up walking home in the dark. The other employees on my shift quickly noticed, and several of them were kind enough to offer me rides home. One night, I rode with Chris' best friend, Coleson. I had caught Coleson looking at me a few times, but he would always smile shyly and turn away. After a few rides home and a little bit of flirting at the store, Coleson asked me to be his girlfriend. I smiled and said yes. Some pretty big things were going on so far in my sophomore year. I had gotten a job, a boyfriend, and was probably out more than I was home. Oh, and since Coleson was a junior, I might even get to go to prom!

What I Learned

If you put forth minimal effort, you'll get minimal results.

Whatever you do, do it enthusiastically,
as something done for the Lord and not for men,
knowing that you will receive the reward
of an inheritance from the Lord.
You serve the Lord Christ. (Colossians 3:23–24)

Girl Talk

1. Are you starting your day by talking to God? What difference do you see in your mood and how you react to things when you've spent time with God versus those days you hurry on without Him?

_____

_____

_____

_____

2. In my new job, I made a decision to be a joyful worker. Are you deciding to have joy in whatever you do, whether it's work, class, sports, or even just being around your family? In what areas do you need to lean on God's strength for joy?

_____

_____

_____

_____

3. Even if you don't realize it, people are watching you. So how can you live your life differently so that your actions and attitude point others to Jesus?

_____

_____

_____

_____

4. How does it change your thinking when you realize you should be doing everything as if you're doing it for God and not for other people or even yourself? Do you believe God can use you in whatever you do?

_____

_____

_____

_____

Chapter 6

Danger! Stay Back

Living on the edge is where it's easiest to slip.

I was really enjoying my new relationship with Coleson. It was such a great feeling to have someone who waited for me after school, who smiled at me while I worked, who called to say hello just because he missed talking to me. Yes, my friends gave me similar attention, but this was different. This was *affection*. This was someone I wanted to have an even deeper relationship with, and we were off to a good start: He was a Christian. We saw each other at work and school. His parents were really nice—even though his dad *did* watch us like a hawk. I got along well with his friends, and he at least knew my friends and was nice to them. I was feeling really good about everything.

This was definitely a more serious relationship for me, especially compared to my crush with Brad. I felt like I had a true boyfriend, and I was ready to put in the effort to make this relationship last. With that, I found myself changing certain things. I would go through several different outfits before going out, and I checked my hair and makeup often. It wasn't unusual for me to try to look nice, but I was definitely making an extra effort. More than that, I caught myself listening to his kind of music, hanging out with his friends, and even going to his church—even though I liked mine better. I wanted to be the perfect girlfriend.

Coleson and I spent a lot of time together. If we didn't have some-where to be, we tended to hang out at his house. It was hard to hang out at mine, because my sister and mom were usually around. Also, our place was really small, so it was difficult for just the two of us to talk. One evening when we were hanging out at Coleson's, he leaned in for a kiss. It felt right, so I leaned in as well. When he kissed me, it didn't feel uncomfortable like it had with Justin. That was our first kiss, and it definitely wouldn't be the last. In fact, the longer I was with Coleson, the more typical it was for us to spend time kissing. Kissing wasn't the only thing we did like it had been in my relationship with Justin; however, we should not have been as passionate as we were. I mean, where was this going? I was too young for marriage, and I *definitely* wasn't ready to have a baby. So, I probably needed to cool it.

Well, hanging out at Coleson's house only seemed to be okay every once in a while. (You know, his dad had those hawk eyes—which was probably a good thing!) It didn't matter, though, because Coleson had a car, and we were always going somewhere. However, the car was also the perfect place to get that long kiss goodnight or a kiss in between going places. Okay, essentially, it was the perfect make-out spot. There, I said it. One of my biggest struggles—aside from the obvious one of being alone at his house—was being in a parked car with Coleson. I admit, having him pick me up and open the car door for me seemed so gentlemanly. On the other hand, the car gave us the opportunity to get physical. I was pushing my boundaries and getting closer and closer to that edge.

Now, I grew up in the mountains of North Carolina, so I was very familiar with looking over the edge of a cliff and thinking, "That's a scary drop I'd never want to take." One of the most popular mountain peaks around is Grandfather Mountain—its ridges look like the profile of an old mountain man's face. Grandfather is famous for its mile-high swinging bridge that connects two of the peaks. My friend Kristy and I once walked across that shaky bridge, but that wasn't what frightened me the most. The most frightening part was on the other side, where the mountain peak consisted mainly of uneven rocks and cliffs—with no guardrail! While Kristy wanted to climb around, all I could think was, *You're crazy to get so close to the edge. What if you fall?*

At least one person has died by getting too close to the edge of Grandfather Mountain and falling. At the Grand Canyon, there is at least one death a year from someone getting too close to the edge. There are warnings and signs posted that say "Danger! Stay back!" But some people ignore them. They think they know what they're doing. Of course, people don't plan to fall; it's just that they get so close to the edge that they slip.

I don't want you to slip and fall. Let my struggles be a warning sign to you. Nothing good comes from being that physical before marriage. I think of the story of David and Bathsheba in 2 Samuel 11–12. To make a long story short, David saw a beautiful woman, asked her over, went too far, got her pregnant, tried to cover it up by having her husband killed, displeased God, and lost the baby.

I think back to David's story and about what he should have done differently. Well, he *definitely* shouldn't have invited a married woman over to hang out. Before that, though, he shouldn't have kept watching her with lustful eyes. But even though David messed up big time, God didn't leave him. He still loved David and gave him another son, Solomon. Jesus later warned His disciples to "Stay awake and pray, so that you won't enter into temptation. The spirit is willing, but the flesh is weak" (Matthew 26:41). That's good advice for all of us. God gives us good brains to know better, and He even gives us the Holy Spirit to guide us away from and out of trouble.

People don't plan to fall; it's just that they get so close to the edge that they slip.

Coleson and I didn't go any farther than kissing (thank goodness), but it still wasn't a good idea to put ourselves in tempting situations. As girls, we usually know what situations to avoid so that we can lessen temptations. For example, if you spend too much money shopping, then you shouldn't hang out at the mall. If you don't want to be tempted to drink or do drugs, then you shouldn't become close friends with people who drink or do drugs. In the same way, if you don't want to go too far physically, you shouldn't be alone with a guy. That may sound a little extreme, but it's the truth. There are tons of places where you can spend time together without interruption, but still have people around you. Having other people around will help you keep your boundaries.

I can look back now and see that there were some ways I could have stayed farther away from the edge. Coleson and I shouldn't have been hanging out at a house without parents around. There were plenty of places in the mall or at coffee shops for us to spend time "alone" together. As for the car, I could have limited the temptation by having a plan for where we were going and being on time getting there. No driving around just to be driving. Then, when leaving for home, I could have called my mom to let her know I was on my way. That way I had accountability to get home and not stop off somewhere. If I still felt like I had to have that kiss goodnight, I should have let Coleson walk me to the door like a gentleman. Even in the movies, the kiss at the door doesn't usually go on forever. I know if I had gotten Coleson to kiss me at the door, it definitely wouldn't have lasted long with my mom watching out the window!

What I Learned

The farther you stay away from the edge, the less likely you'll be to go over.

So, whoever thinks he stands must be careful not to fall. No temptation has overtaken you except what is common to humanity. God is faithful, and He will not allow you to be tempted beyond what you are able, but with the temptation He will also provide a way of escape so that you are able to bear it.
(1 Corinthians 10:12–13)

Tips to Avoid Dating Danger

- Write down your commitment to stay pure. Share it with your parents and friends, telling them why it's important to you to wait.

- Have a plan to protect your purity and make sure the guy agrees to it. (For example: We will not be in a room by ourselves behind a closed door.)

- Groups are great! You have automatic accountability plus a better balance in your relationships.

- Spend time doing activities that build your friendship. Romance comes and goes, but friendship is a great foundation.

Girl Talk

1. What do you think about the way I changed some of my habits because I was trying to impress the guy I was dating? Have you done the same?

_____

_____

_____

_____

2. What do you think my focus was during this time in my life? Did my life seem out of balance? What's your focus right now? Does everything revolve around one thing (that isn't God)? Or is your life balanced with other people and things?

_____

_____

_____

_____

3. Do you know where the edge is? Try this: instead of asking how far you can go and stay *pure*, ask yourself how far you can go and stay *holy*. What's your answer?

_____

_____

_____

_____

4. Can you think of ways to prevent or lessen those temptations that come up in your life? Are there friends who will keep you accountable?

_____

_____

_____

5. Do you feel really guilty for the things you struggle with? Remember, everyone struggles, and you can turn to Jesus for help and forgiveness. Read 1 John 1:7–9. How does this make you feel?

_____

_____

_____

_____

Chapter 7

Is That a Speck in Your Eye?

I'm not like that . . . am I?

My relationship with Coleson lasted about two to three months. Really long relationship, huh? He broke up with me because one of his old crushes started flirting with him once we started dating. Coleson had talked *a lot* about how much this girl got on his nerves. It wasn't until later that I found out Coleson had liked her for a long time, before we had even met. His jealousy was the reason he kept mentioning her. Sadly, even though this girl had been flirting with him, it turned out that she didn't really want to date Coleson—she just didn't want anyone else to date him either. She was just that kind of girl—the kind who plays with guys' hearts and treats dating like a game. How mean!

I guess I was on the rebound a little after Coleson. I liked having a boyfriend. It made me feel special and loved. But there were plenty of other fish in the sea, and I was sure I could replace him. Maybe he'd even get a little jealous if I found someone else. I wasn't going to let this break-up get me down. I was going to act like it didn't matter—and now I had the freedom to have fun and flirt with other guys.

I was still working at the grocery store. Since I wasn't dating Coleson, other people would drive me home at night. One was a guy named Matt. He had the kindest heart—you could just tell. We went to a movie once, and he surprised me with a kiss. But while we talked and flirted a little, we never really dated. He was nice, but there weren't any real sparks for me.

She was just that kind of girl—the kind who plays with guys' hearts and treats dating like a game.

Walking down the hall at school one day, I paused to say hi to Matt. Next to him was a guy I had never met. We made eye contact and both kind of smirked—there were definitely sparks. He was one of Matt's friends, but he didn't work at the grocery store or come to the morning devotionals. I was intrigued by this new mystery guy. We didn't have a chance to talk since class was starting, but I hoped to bump into him again.

Soon after that, I did bump into him and was officially introduced. His name was Evan. Over the next couple of weeks, I ended up in detention a few days after school. Long story, but I had to make up hours because I had missed too many classes. I promise I'll come back to that and explain. For now, I will go ahead and admit that I was not perfect by any means. Anyway, I was in detention and guess who walked in? Yep, it was Evan. We both smiled and looked puzzled to see each other there. We weren't allowed to talk, so we passed notes back and forth.

Okay, so why was I in detention? Well, I can never leave Jason out as a big part of my high school life—and he was the reason I was in detention. Well, part of the reason. He was still my best guy friend, even though he was constantly trying to get me to date him. Oh, don't feel bad for him, though—he was always dating someone himself. But no matter who we were dating, we still seemed to be getting into something together. This year, we had P.E. and Geography together. Well, Geography was easy, and it was also at the same time that several of our friends had lunch. So Jason and I sometimes skipped class and had two lunches. It worked out well until Kristy's mom, who was a teacher at the high school, saw us at different lunches. Busted!

Well, after detention, I started to hang out with Evan a lot more, and Matt definitely took notice. In fact, Matt began spreading rumors about me at school. He said I liked to get around and that I used guys. It seems that Matt thought I had been interested in him *and* flirting with another guy too. His feelings were hurt, and he was mad at me for leading him on. Oh no! Had I played games with Matt's heart just like the girl had done with Coleson's?

I went to Matt immediately and told him that it was not my intention to lead him on. I told him I thought he was a great guy, and I enjoyed hanging out with him, but I just wanted to be friends. I did let him know that I liked Evan—I wanted to be honest about that. He forgave me, and we stayed friends. The rumors stopped and things went back to normal.

You know, I must not have been so innocent if I hurt a guy like Matt—especially enough for him to start rumors about me. I guess I had been playing the dating game a little, too, and was just enjoying the attention. But in the end someone got hurt.

What I Learned

Don't look at someone else and tell yourself, "I'm not *that* bad." Look at Jesus and ask, "Am I really *that* good?"

Why do you look at the speck in your brother's eye but don't notice the log in your own eye? (Matthew 7:3)

Girl Talk

1. Why do you think I wanted a boyfriend so badly after breaking up with Coleson? Why do you think girls want a "boyfriend" sometimes instead of a "boy friend?"

_____

_____

_____

_____

2. Are you looking for a relationship for the right reasons? What would the right reasons be for dating someone?

_____

_____

_____

3. Have you ever played with someone's emotions only for your benefit? It doesn't have to be with a guy; it could be with friends or family too. Do you think someone will eventually call you on it? How is your manipulation going to affect your relationship?

_____

_____

_____

_____

4. What does Matthew 7:3 mean to you?

_____

_____

_____

_____

Chapter 8

Did Someone Say Prom?

Sometimes fun memories are made in the most unexpected places.

❧❧❧❧❧❧❧❧❧❧❧❧

Evan and I continued to see each other here and there around school. Though our days of detention had been served, he would still give me a ride home every once in a while. He was also a pretty easy guy to talk to, and we continued to learn about each other little by little. Now, we weren't dating by any means, but we were enjoying our friendship. Okay, maybe we were flirting with the idea of dating, but there was no need to rush into anything. I had tried that before!

After a while, there was some talk going around school that Evan was thinking of asking me to the prom. *Oh my goodness! That would be so awesome!* And as prom got closer, I was really hoping the rumors were true. One day at the end of lunch, Evan said he had something to ask me. I held my breath. Could this be it? *Yes!* He asked me to prom! Regrettably, I turned him down. *Just kidding!* Of course, I said yes! *Wahoo!* I was only a sophomore, but I was going to prom! I couldn't focus on anything else the rest of the day. I had to tell my friends, tell my mom, and *get a dress!*

But prom wasn't the only good news that year. At the same time I was creating this new friendship with Evan, I got to reconnect with an old friend. My great friend from middle school, Jessica, had moved to Texas right before high school started. But now she was moving back and was only about an hour and a half away from me. Because we had kept in touch with letters and phone calls, we were still good friends. We soon started making plans to see each other over the weekends. Luckily, Jessica's mom was willing to pick me up since I didn't have my driver's license yet and my mom couldn't drive because of a severe degeneration in her eyes. I was really excited about seeing my good friend again.

There was one weekend in particular that I was really looking forward to. That weekend Jessica and her brother were inviting some friends from their school over. Because her brother, Steven, was only a year older, their friends all ended up hanging out together. They were a really fun crowd, and I seemed to fit in pretty well. We played basketball and Ping-Pong and watched a movie. The whole day of hanging out was great, but it definitely felt different somehow. I had always thought of Steven as the annoying older brother, but this time, I didn't feel so annoyed. On the contrary, I was having a lot of fun with Steven—almost to the point of being flirty!

Everyone stayed late that night watching TV, but slowly people began to go home. Then, eventually, Jessica said she was going to bed. Oddly, I didn't want to go to bed yet and stayed up with Steven watching TV. Each time one of us would get up to get something to drink or go to the bathroom, we would sit back down just a little closer to each other. Soon we were side by side. We started talking and just kept talking . . . and talking . . . and talking. We stayed up the entire night talking! I'd never had so much fun talking to a guy. We didn't want people to think we were crazy, though, for staying up all night—especially since it was just the two of us. So when we heard Jessica and her parents get up, Steven ran to his room and got into his bed. I lay down on the couch and pretended I fell asleep there. I mean, this was the brother of one of my best friends, and I didn't know what she would think. Actually, I wasn't sure what was going on myself. I just know we had a great time hanging out, and I didn't want it to end. On the drive home, I couldn't help wondering if Steven had felt a connection like I did.

It wasn't long before I got an answer. One night, Jessica called, sounding pretty excited. She said Steven wanted me to go to their Junior/ Senior with him—this was their school's equivalent of a prom. Jessica and Steven went to a Christian school that didn't have a traditional prom with dancing. Still, I would be able to dress up and hang out with Steven and Jessica. I didn't hesitate. I told her I would love to go. Two proms! Thank goodness they were different weekends.

As I waited for the proms and searched for a dress, normal life went on. My weeks were busy with school, work, and church, but I also started doing some new things. I heard about something new called Young Life, which was an organization where Christian college students mentored high school students. There was going to be a meeting every week, usually at someone's house. The first meeting, though, started in the school parking lot. After short introductions, they divided us into teams for a scavenger hunt of sorts. Each team was given a penny and had one hour to go around town and trade the penny for something bigger and better. Then we were all to meet up to compare what we had gotten. Wow! This wasn't what I'd expected from a Christian meeting, but it sure was a fun start. Carol Ann and Kristy were on my team. At the end of the trading, some teams had gotten some much bigger things, but we were super-pumped about what we ended up with. When it was our team's turn to present, one of the guys opened his hands to reveal . . . a white mouse! We had gotten it from the pet store in the mall. It was funny to see people's reactions.

I continued to go to Young Life and had more fun than I would have ever expected. The meetings usually included Bible studies, singing praise and worship songs, skits (both funny and serious), games, and just hanging out and getting to know one another. It was a blast! I learned that I could live *a life of worship*—not just worship at church. Jason, Evan, and some other friends heard about the fun we had at Young Life and started coming too.

Even with my busy schedule, I found time to go dress shopping. We only had two formal stores in town, so it was slim pickings. Though it took a lot of effort and alterations, I did finally find the perfect dress. It was a classic, long, black formal dress with white accents. I couldn't wait to wear it!

Steven's prom came first. As Jessica and I got ready, I was excited, but also a little disappointed because they didn't allow dancing. Honestly, I thought the Junior/Senior sounded a little lame. But, I told myself, I was getting to dress up and go out with a guy I really enjoyed being with.

At first, the night was pretty typical—pictures followed by a dinner and entertainment. What I hadn't realized, though, was that the school had planned a whole night of activities in place of dancing. We changed out of our dresses and the whole prom crowd went out. First, we went rolling skating, then we played laser tag (where I used Steven as a human body shield), and then we all went to a classmate's house for more food and a movie. (At one point, Steven and I secretly held hands. I think we were mostly worried about what Jessica would think.) Well, things came to an end around seven in the morning. It had been the longest, most fun event I had ever been to. Honestly, an evening that I thought would be lame, ended up being one of the best nights of my life!

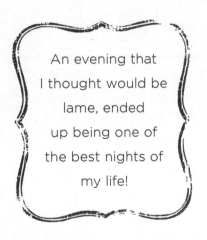

An evening that I thought would be lame, ended up being one of the best nights of my life!

Soon after that, it was time for prom number two. Evan picked me up and my mom took pictures, but I really don't have as many memories of this prom. I know there were decorations, food, and music for dancing. It was nice being with Evan, and of course I loved being dressed up. Overall, it was what I expected a prom to be, but now it paled in comparison to the fun I'd had at Steven's Junior/Senior. Who knew I'd have more fun at a potentially uptight Christian school's event than at a prom?

As I look back, that sophomore year was one of amazing memories. All of those great moments had one thing in common: they were all with people who loved Jesus. As I had learned at Young Life, I didn't have to love God only at church. God is in His people, and He will bless the time we spend together. I would have missed out on His blessings, though, if I hadn't tried new things, made an effort to be a friend, and chosen to take advantage of the wonderful opportunities I was given.

What I Learned

The greatest memories are made by intentionally making time to create them with the people you love. So take hold of this year and make the most of it!

❧

If we walk in the light as He Himself is in the light, we have fellowship with one another, and the blood of Jesus His Son cleanses us from all sin. (1 John 1:7)

Girl Talk

1. It took effort to keep in touch with Jessica when she moved away, but look at the blessings that came from it. Are you putting effort into your friendships—whether near or far? What could you do to be a better friend? (Proverbs 18:24 is a great verse to stick in your back pocket.)

_____

_____

_____

_____

2. Just like my nontraditional prom and Young Life game nights, what are some activities you can do with friends that are "outside the box?" Think scavenger hunts, game nights, craft parties, dinner parties, disco parties, or going to local festivals, Christian concerts, and events. Be creative!

_____

_____

_____

_____

3. Do you think hanging out and having fun with other Christians can help your relationship with God? How?

_____

_____

_____

_____

4. Read 1 John 1:6 aloud, and then read verse 7. What are the differences in the two verses? Where are you hanging out? In the light or in the dark?

_____

_____

_____

_____

Chapter 9

Waiting to Wear the Dress

There's a purpose and a place for everything.

As I think back about how excited I was to go to prom, I ponder what it was I was so excited about. For me, it was one of few opportunities I would have to get dressed up. Not just to look nice, but to really go all out. It was partially the hair and makeup, but more than anything else, it came down to the dress. It was the dress that would make me feel beautiful. I think of fairy tales and how amazing those royal balls looked with all the gorgeous gowns. It was a time for the girl to shine and the guy to sweep her off of her feet—and I was all about that!

The dress I had chosen for prom was very valuable to me, and I didn't want anything to happen to it before that special night. It hung on the back of my door, covered by a clear dress bag. I would often glance over at it, filled with anticipation and excitement for the day I would finally get to wear it.

But what if I had gotten impatient and decided to go ahead and wear the dress? I mean, it was beautiful, it made me feel good to wear it, and it was right there in front of me. Maybe I could wear it to school, to work, to the movies, or on a walk.

Of course, you and I know that would have been ridiculous. Just because I *could* have worn the dress, doesn't mean I *should* have. I could have messed it up or gotten it dirty, and those weren't appropriate settings for wearing a dress such as this. This dress was for prom and nothing less than that.

But isn't this what some people do? They get impatient and can't wait to wear the dress, or maybe they don't value it as highly as they should. The sad thing is, if they had only waited, they would find that the royal ball was just around the corner—the place the dress was made for and the place where it would shine as it was meant to. You see, it's all about its purpose and place.

God has a purpose and a place for intimacy between a man and a woman. It's something special to share in marriage and to strengthen a couple's bond together. Your purity is the most beautiful dress you will ever own. It's not meant for just any old day or just any relationship. It's meant for that big day when you say "I do" and make a commitment to the man you love.

Your purity is the most beautiful dress you will ever own.

In Matthew 19:4–6, Jesus answers a question about divorce, but for me, it helps me see how God views marriage. It says that a man and woman leave their parents and become one flesh, not to be separated. The two become one. Sex is *not* for someone you think you like. It's part of a marriage, a bond, and a commitment. It ties you not just physically to that person, but emotionally and spiritually as well.

So what if you have worn your dress before it was intended? What if you made some mistakes that you can't take back? What now? In John 8:1–11, the scribes and Pharisees brought a woman before Jesus who was caught having sex with someone she was not married to. The law of that time said she should be stoned until dead. The scribes and Pharisees asked Jesus what they should do. They hoped to trap Him in a bad answer, but Jesus said, "The one without sin among you should be the first to throw a stone at her." One by one, the men left. Why? Because each of them had sin in their lives—just as each of us do. Jesus then said to the woman, "Neither do I condemn you. . . . Go and from now on do not sin anymore."

So what does that mean for you? First, realize that we all mess up, and that's why we all need Jesus. Then, ask Him for forgiveness, and go and live following Jesus, asking for His help every day.

You see, we all have different stories to tell and different ways that God can take our past and use it to help us—and others—grow. Every person's story is valuable and useful to God. One person may think her story isn't worth sharing because she didn't go through something awful, while another person may think her life can't be used because of her awful past. Both are lies of Satan to keep us from living the full life God has planned for us. Once we decide to live for Jesus, we can have victory over sin. We can then live an abundant life and help others to as well.

What I Learned

My purity is valuable enough to save and protect. Therefore, I'll wait with anticipation for God's perfect plan.

I greatly rejoice in the LORD, I exult in my God; for He has clothed me with the garments of salvation and wrapped me in a robe of righteousness, as a groom wears a turban and as a bride adorns herself with her jewels. (Isaiah 61:10)

Girl Talk

1. Do you think God is trying to keep something good from you by saying you should wait until marriage to have sex? Why do you think He says to wait? What does He want for you?

_____

_____

_____

2. If I went to all that trouble to protect a dress for a special dance, then how much more should I protect my purity for the day I get married? Can you see its purpose is meant for a specific time and place to shine?

_____

_____

_____

3. If God designed sex to supernaturally bind two people together, never to be separated, then what do you think happens when you don't wait for your husband? If sex is the glue for marriage, what happens if you use it for a short-term fling? What could the emotional, spiritual, and physical effects be in your relationships, both in the present and in the future?

_____

_____

_____

4. Do you ever feel like your sins are worse than someone else's? Read John 8:1–11. Can you see that no one should be throwing stones because we all need Jesus' forgiveness? In what areas do you need to ask Jesus to help you leave your sin behind and start living the fuller life He has for you? (Read 2 Corinthians 5:17.)

_____

_____

_____

5. Are you willing to choose a life of purity? Why or why not? Talk with your girlfriends about what the outcomes of waiting could be versus the outcomes of not waiting.

_____

_____

_____

_____

Chapter 10

Torn

How do you follow your heart when
it's going two different directions?

Well, the proms were over, but both guys were still in the picture. I wasn't exclusively dating either one, and Evan and Steven each knew about the other. At this point, I was just friends with both of them. Of course, I saw Evan around school, and he would sometimes swing by my work. Other times, he made it to Young Life. Seeing Steven took a lot more effort since he was out of town. When I did see him, though, it was over a weekend, so we had more quality time.

I found ways to go to Jessica's whenever I could, both to see her and Steven. I even talked Jason into taking a road trip there. He had never met Jessica or Steven before. It was interesting to see my best guy friend interact with a guy I potentially liked. They were both nice, but there was this underlying tone of competition, since they both liked me in some way.

That night, as we were all heading to the couch to watch TV, there was the unspoken question of who I would sit next to—Jason or Steven. I decided to play it safe and sat next to Jessica. She still didn't realize I liked her brother, though I think Jason could tell. Really, I still questioned whether or not Steven liked me, or if he was just having fun hanging out. *Oh, please let it be that he liked me!*

I was kind of torn between my feelings for Steven and my feelings for Evan. They were both really nice, both Christians, and I enjoyed their company. I kept finding myself, though, wanting the time to never end when I was with Steven. Then, one night back at home, I received an unexpected call from Jessica. She sounded really giddy as she told me that Steven wanted to talk to me. Steven and I had *never* talked on the phone before, so I knew something was up. Steven asked me to be his girlfriend. So he *did* like me! I said yes, of course! Jessica later said she had never seen Steven this excited about a girl before.

Steven and I talked on the phone and visited when we could. On our weekends together, we would stay up all night just to talk. We went for late-night cappuccino runs, played Ping-Pong, and watched crazy old movies. One night he pretended to stumble close to me, but I knew he wanted to kiss me. I leaned over, and it was such a sweet kiss. He was wonderful, and I'd never had so much fun hanging out with a boyfriend.

That summer after my sophomore year, Steven went to Africa on a mission trip. He sent me a postcard and a necklace, which was so thoughtful and romantic. However, I was sad that I wasn't getting to see him, and the long distance started taking a bit of a toll on me. To make matters more complicated, I was seeing Evan around all the time. I knew he still liked me and, to even add a little more pressure, one of the Young Life leaders started saying I should give Evan a chance. Slowly I broke down and gave in to the guy who was right there in front of me. I called Steven to let him know. I hated hurting him, but I had made my choice.

Evan and I were now exclusive. We hung out the whole rest of the summer and into our junior year. Evan seemed to always make the extra effort to be considerate and make sure I was happy. In the car, he would let me pick the music I wanted to listen to. I found out later that he liked rap, but he never played it around me because he knew I hated it. He even asked if I wanted to take turns going to each other's churches. Then he started making an effort to get to know my friends. Looking back, it was kind of the opposite of my relationship with Coleson.

The longer I was with Evan, the more comfortable I got with him. We were inseparable and did everything together. It felt like a real relationship and was definitely my longest one so far. Evan and I went to the Homecoming Dance together, we said "I love you," and he even bought me a ring. Don't freak out! It wasn't a wedding ring, but it was very special. But the more time we spent together, the more physical our relationship turned. We had kissed before, but it became more often. I began to feel really guilty about how we were with each other. I wanted us to go back to how we were before, but Evan didn't seem to want that. It was like once those feelings were turned on, there was no going back.

Argh! Why was this happening again? I'd just wanted a little romance, but now I felt like Evan was no longer interested in me as a person. Again, I knew where I stood on not having sex, and Evan never asked for that, but I also knew that this was not heading down the best path for me. In my frustration, I began to think about Steven. We had had so much fun together and enjoyed each other's company. Even though I did kiss Steven every once in a while, that wasn't what our relationship was based on. Had I made a really big mistake?

Evan started spending less time with me and more time hanging out with his friends. I heard they tried drinking, and suddenly it seemed that Evan's whole demeanor changed. In his frustration with me, his true colors came out. He started blasting his music and playing songs with content I didn't like at all. He was now this kind of bad boy, and I didn't go for bad boys. After being out of town one weekend, I called him. He sounded messed up and not himself. I didn't know what was going on, but I think he had been out with another girl. Wow, this was not what I bargained for. Where was the kind, loving guy I had started dating, or had he just been a big phony?

Do not be deceived: "Bad company corrupts good morals." —1 Corinthians 15:33

Evan and I broke up, and it was really hard. Evan kept trying to work it out, but I felt like I had been deceived. I realized I had been the one trying to make him be a good person and, ultimately, that was not my job. I could care about Evan and pray for him, but I didn't need to be pulled down with him. I needed to let him go. I needed a guy who could lift me up and who went to church, not for me, but because he wanted to. I needed someone who was spiritually mature, and someone who was definitely for real.

I went by Evan's work one day and asked someone at the front desk to give him something—it was a box that held the ring. As I drove away, I saw Evan in the rearview mirror, running after me. I took a deep breath and pulled away without looking back. I never heard from Evan again.

What I Learned

Your emotions can blind you to the truth. Be careful not to be deceived by them.

The heart is more deceitful than anything else, and incurable—who can understand it? (Jeremiah 17:9)

Girl Talk

1. Just as I tried to be someone I wasn't for Coleson, Evan tried to be someone he wasn't for me. Have you ever tried to be something you aren't just to please someone else? How far do you think that will get you? What could be the results?

_____

_____

_____

_____

2. Do you think I should have stayed with Evan and helped him work through his struggles? Read 1 Corinthians 15:33 and 2 Corinthians

6:14–15. Can you really change someone? Or are you just standing in the way of them reaching out to the One who can change them?

_____

_____

_____

_____

3. It was hard to say no to Evan when he pleaded to get back together. My heart wanted to stay, but my head told me no way. What are the dangers of "just following your heart" like the world says? Since Jeremiah 17:9 says you can't trust your heart, whose voice should you listen to?

_____

_____

_____

_____

4. Dating relationships can tend to be more physical than relational after a while. Why do you think that is? How can you keep a relationship focused on the right things? What are those right things?

_____

_____

_____

_____

Chapter 11

Dating Outside the Box

So how should a daughter of the King date?

Boy, this dating business was hard! The guy in front of me was not who he claimed to be, and the guy I enjoyed spending time with was never around. As I second-guessed letting go of Steven, I realized I had lacked the true commitment needed to make a long-distance relationship work. But then, should I be committed to making a relationship work at sixteen? I wasn't married yet; I was only dating. So it got me to thinking: How should I view dating, and how did others?

From my experience, dating tended to be a relationship you stayed in until one party was no longer interested or happy, or when it took too much work. Huh, that doesn't sound very appealing; nevertheless, it's pretty accurate. Dating is a very temporary state that can sometimes lead to something greater, or it can lead to confusion, break-ups, and heart-ache. Some people see dating as a free make-out pass (like Justin). Some see it as an esteem booster. Others are only interested if it's easy. Some will use it as a security blanket so that at least they're not alone. And then there are those who see it as an opportunity to get to know another person. Ah, that sounds better. Time spent getting to know someone.

It had started out that way with both Evan and Steven. Things only changed when I added the label of dating. For Steven and me, dating added a pressure to be committed to someone who wasn't even around half the time. At that point in my life, I was too immature for that kind of commitment. When presented with the choice of a close, easy relationship or a long-distance one, I took the easier route. But dating Evan then became my "security blanket." I took him everywhere I went, and he made me feel comfortable. That is, until he took the security blanket and started smothering me with it. Thankfully, I was able to see who Evan really was—someone who only pretended to be the guy I would like.

Dating is an opportune time to let another person see who you really are, but a lot of people don't feel free to be themselves, flaws and all. So when they start dating, they also tend to start acting. It's as if they were asked to play the lead in a love story. So what happens when they get tired of pretending? Believe me, it's an awful feeling to find out your relationship is a façade. It's never good to pretend to be someone you're not. After all, we all have our quirks and differences. That's what makes us unique. Who you are is not something to hide. It's something to embrace!

> Who you are is not something to hide. It's something to embrace!

Okay, I had *my* thoughts on what dating should be, but I was really curious about what the Bible had to say. For the fun of it, I searched for the word "dating" in my Bible. As I suspected, dating is not even mentioned in the Bible. My next thought, then, was to see how the love stories in the Bible came to be. One of the most popular is the story of Ruth and Boaz.

Ruth and her mother-in-law, Naomi, were both widowed. Instead of returning to her own family, Ruth chose to stay by Naomi's side. She spent her days humbly gathering leftover grain from the fields of Boaz, a relative of Naomi. Boaz noticed Ruth's selfless dedication (Ruth 2:11–12) and was kind to her. Eventually Ruth (with a little push from Naomi) asked Boaz to take her as his wife and this was his response:

> May the LORD bless you, my daughter. You have shown more kindness now than before, because you have not pursued younger men, whether rich or poor. Now don't be afraid, my daughter. I will do for you whatever you say, since all the people in my town know that you are a woman of noble character. (Ruth 3:10–11)

Boaz did marry Ruth. And later, they had a son named Obed—who had a son named Jesse, who had a son named David, who became a great king.

Hmm, I don't really see any "dating" going on between Ruth and Boaz. So how did Ruth get such a great guy? And how did Boaz know what he was getting into if he hadn't dated her? Well, Boaz actually knew a lot about Ruth, because her reputation had preceded her. He saw how hard she worked and how she cared for Naomi, and he knew she didn't chase after other men. Though Ruth had caught Boaz's eye as she worked in the fields, it was her humility and love for others that kept his interest.

Another love story is found in Genesis 24—the story of Isaac and Rebekah. Abraham prayed for God to provide a wife for his son, Isaac. In faith, Abraham sent a servant to find her, and in faith, the servant prayed for God to reveal her to him. God answered both men's prayers in Rebekah. Then, in faith, Rebekah traveled back to meet her future husband, a man she had never met before. Isaac and Rebekah married and shared a love that came from God. Through their children two great nations would come.

What? Wait a minute! Isaac and Rebekah had never even met? How crazy is that? But how awesome would that be, though, to know that God was the one who brought you and your spouse together? And what faith to let God choose your mate!

Okay . . . well my dating relationships sound kind of lame now. I had never *not* worried about finding a boyfriend and had never focused my attention only on helping others. I certainly had never expected God to just tell me, "Here's the one." Times have changed, right? God probably doesn't work the same way to create amazing relationships . . . or does He? Well, the Bible does say He's the same yesterday, today, and forever (Hebrews 13:8). *Hmm.*

As I continued my search for what dating should be, I started hearing a few couples around church say they were "courting." I was intrigued. What was the difference? Surely, they weren't talking about hanging out on their parents' front porches! So I asked. These couples explained to me that their relationship was based on getting to know someone that they could potentially marry. They wanted God to be at the center of their relationship, and they sought His guidance. They were also committed to not having sex before marriage. In spending time together, they would only hang out in group settings with friends or family.

At the time, I thought courting sounded old-fashioned and maybe just a little extreme. However, now knowing that those same couples have been happily married for years, I decided to revisit the concept. So I turned to the Merriam-Webster online dictionary and looked up "dating." Funny, "dating" wouldn't come up for me there. I guess it's even too difficult for the dictionary folks to put a finger on. Next, I tried "boyfriend." Merriam-Webster defines *boyfriend* as "a male friend" or "a frequent or regular male companion in a romantic or sexual relationship." "Court" then is "to engage in social activities leading to engagement and marriage." Definitely two different approaches to relationships—and one sounds a lot healthier than the other.

While I never used the term "courting," I did like the overall concept. It was maybe a little outside the box, but God doesn't have to work inside our box. His ways of bringing people together are bigger and more meaningful. After Evan, I knew I wanted more than ever to have a godly relationship that could one day lead to marriage. I wasn't sure exactly what that would look like for me or how to get it; but I knew it was out there.

What I Learned

Whether you "date," "court," or "go out," having God at the center of your relationship makes all the difference.

"For My thoughts are not your thoughts, and your ways are not My ways." This is the LORD'S declaration. "For as heaven is higher than earth, so My ways are higher than your ways, and My thoughts than your thoughts." (Isaiah 55:8–9)

Girl Talk

1. How would you define dating? What have you seen come from dating—both the good and the bad?

_____

_____

_____

_____

2. What do you think about the definition of courting that those couples gave me? Does it change the way you view dating? How would your relationship change if you had these guidelines as your standard?

_____

_____

_____

_____

3. I don't think we should get caught up in the words "dating" or "courting" so much as the actual intention of the relationship. What are your intentions for a relationship? Is keeping God at its center one of them? If you currently have a boyfriend, do you know what his intentions are?

_____

_____

_____

_____

4. Read both love stories—the book of Ruth and Genesis 24. What insights do you feel God is giving you on relationships and marriage?

_____

_____

_____

_____

Chapter 12

Carol Ann Shines

The most beautiful light shines from the inside out.

Have you ever had times in your life when things just didn't seem to go your way? Times when you wanted to whine and complain that life's not fair? Then, you finally realize that the world doesn't revolve around your being happy—and maybe it's time to grow up. Well, that describes the end of my junior year. Things definitely hadn't gone as planned. I'd once been in my own happy bubble of a relationship, but that bubble had popped. I was now taking a look at the rest of the world around me. My friends had continued on with their lives. They had their own interests and places they fit in. For the first time in a while, I felt out of place and a little alone. As I looked at the others around me in relationships, I realized I no longer had my security blanket. It was just me, and I wasn't sure how to handle it.

I had been used to either having a boyfriend or having someone pursue me, but now there was no one. Even Jason—who'd never stopped asking me out—was kind of giving me the cold shoulder. I realized, though, that I hadn't given him much time while I was dating Evan.

Jason was frustrated with me, and this was his way of showing it. Honestly, several of my friends probably felt the same way.

Ironically, once I stopped dating, it seemed that everyone else started. Jason was dating someone, Kristy was dating someone, and several friends from church had recently gotten into serious relationships too. Then, there was Carol Ann.

Carol Ann was my best friend. She had watched me go from one guy to another, but had never dated herself. She had stayed home, while I went off to two different proms. But things were changing for Carol Ann. She was now getting attention from this really nice guy on the baseball team. Not only that, but she seemed to have befriended everybody. I was amazed at how many people she talked to as we walked down the hall. And she was suddenly glowing with this amazing confidence.

That year, Carol Ann went to not one, but *two* proms—while it seemed I would be the one staying home. The tables were completely turned on me. No boyfriend and no prom. This is where I so desperately wanted to whine, "Not fair!" However, I knew I needed to grow up and be happy for Carol Ann. And I *was* happy for her. Maybe a tad jealous and still a little sad for myself, but I really did want great things for her. It was her turn to shine and my time to sit on the sidelines.

Still, I was puzzled by the changes in my friend and wondered what had made such a big difference. Before, *I* had been the confident one—mostly because of the guys who liked me. But Carol Ann's confidence happened before she knew that a guy liked her and before she started making more friends. If her confidence wasn't coming from a guy or popularity, where was it coming from?

The more I watched Carol Ann, the more I wanted to understand where her confident glow was coming from. One night, while sleeping over at Carol Ann's house, I saw that she was reading her Bible in bed. I asked if that was something she always did. She said yes, it was something she chose to do every night. Now honestly, I love God, but back then I hated reading. So unfortunately, my Bible tended to go unopened except at church.

I also noticed a difference in Carol Ann at church. When we would sing, she would lift up her hands and face, close her eyes, and sing with all she had. She didn't care what others were doing. She just focused on loving and worshipping God. That's when it clicked—it was her love for God that was making the difference! Carol Ann not only loved Him, she was also willing to work at getting to know Him and having a better relationship with Him. I understood now! Her security in God gave her the joy and confidence to be happy in her own skin. That's what made Carol Ann shine!

Her security in God gave her the joy and confidence to be happy in her own skin.

When you shine like Carol Ann, it's not because of your hairstyle or clothes or makeup. It's not because you're popular or have a boyfriend. It's because God is in your heart. You shine from the inside out and people see that.

God's love is so amazing that it transforms who we are and how we act. Matthew 5:14–16 says that our light was meant to shine and not be hidden. It should shine in everything we do. When others see that light in you, it helps them see Jesus. The Bible describes it this way: "For you were once darkness, but now you are light in the Lord. Walk as children of light—for the fruit of the light results in all goodness, righteousness, and truth" (Ephesians 5:8–10). And since God's joy doesn't come from our circumstances or status, but from within, we can have a joy and a hope even when times are hard.

Now that I knew why Carol Ann was always beaming, I wanted that for myself. I realized I needed a closer relationship with God. If only I had put the same effort into my relationship with God as I had put into my search for a boyfriend! This was my time to grow and to be molded into who God would have me to be. I wanted to shine!

Little did I realize that God had already put me in a great place to start learning some valuable lessons. That year I had signed up for a class called Industrial Arts. We worked on several customized projects using materials such as leather, stone, and clay, but it was the clay that really taught me about God.

Clay, of course, is so very moldable. At first, we just worked it with our hands to roll, flatten, and score it together to create things. Then, our teacher gave us special stains to paint with. The stains didn't look very good, though, and half the time you couldn't even see the color. But once the pieces were fired in the oven, the colors became bright, glossy, and beautiful—and the clay pieces themselves became much stronger than before.

Later, we worked with clay on the potter's wheel. The clay had to be in the perfect center of the wheel—otherwise, it would fall when you tried to bring it up and shape it. Also, your hands had to be perfectly steady, pulling evenly and gradually—or again it would fall. The clay tested my patience, and I had to start over many times. I thought being in control of the wheel would be easy, but I was wrong. It took someone much better than me to make a masterpiece.

In Jeremiah 18, God tells us that He is the potter, and we are the clay. After working with clay, I understand why He compared us to clay. Clay has the potential to be so many wonderful things. It can go from a big ole mess to something beautiful and useful when sculpted by a master potter. And each piece is unique; no two will be alike. Before the potter can begin, though, the clay must be centered where he wants it to be. Finally, it is put through the fire, which makes the finished piece stronger and more beautiful.

You see, if life were too easy and we had no struggles, we wouldn't feel the need to turn to God. By going through the fires of hard times, we can come out stronger and shining more beautifully than ever before. Just like the colors on the pottery shone. Just like Carol Ann shone. So even though my year hadn't gone as planned, I was right where God wanted me to be—right where He could mold me.

What I Learned

When I'm in the center of God's will, I am moldable. When I go through fires, they make me stronger and more beautiful. And the more I seek God, the more He will shine in me.

In the same way, let your light shine before men,
so that they may see your good works and give glory
to your Father in heaven. (Matthew 5:16)

Girl Talk

1. God desires a deeper relationship with you. Read Romans 8:35–39. Could times of loneliness or trials be opportunities to grow closer to Him and shine more brightly than before? Who or what has been standing in your way of a deeper relationship with God?

_____

_____

_____

_____

2. To have that joy that shines from within and allows you to be comfortable in your own skin, you can't find your identity in others, in your appearance, or in your talents, but in how God sees you. Read Psalm 139:13–18, 1 Samuel 16:7, Genesis 1:27, 1 John 3:1, 1 Peter 3:3–4, and 1 Corinthians 3:16–17. What truths do you see and what lies should you stop believing about yourself?

_____

_____

_____

_____

3. Have you been letting your Bible go untouched? Read 2 Timothy 3:16–17. God's Word equips you for life. Find a Bible reading plan—on the Internet or through your church—and start reading. It's okay if you don't get everything at first; the Holy Spirit will start showing you things. Don't be afraid to ask questions. What's your plan?

_____

_____

_____

_____

4. I was in a bubble when I was dating Evan. I let my friends and family fall by the side. Who or what have you been neglecting because you are consumed with a guy (or sports, TV, school, or a job)? How can you start prioritizing better?

_____

_____

_____

_____

5. What do you think would happen if you sought out a deeper relationship with God above anything else this year?

_____

_____

_____

_____

Chapter 13

Spring Break!

Sometimes you've just got to get away to see things clearly.

It had been a tough year, so thank goodness I had spring break to look forward to! No, not the kind with bikinis and parties—I wasn't a "party" girl, remember. And I wasn't heading to the beach; I was heading to the mountains. Carol Ann, Jason, Jessica, and I had made plans with some of our Young Life leaders to go to Windy Gap, a Young Life camp. There were cabins, a big lake, an obstacle course, a climbing wall, and . . . *the Blob*. The Blob was a large inflatable out on the lake with a wooden platform rising high up behind it. One person would sit on the edge of the Blob, while another person jumped from the platform— bouncing the first person as high and far as possible. A guy twice my size bounced me off the Blob, and I shot up like a rocket, with tons of air time before landing in the lake. Now that was a crazy—and pretty awesome—start to the trip!

Camp was amazing. In between the skits, discussions about God, and fun activities with friends, the leaders would push for us to break away and find a spot outside by ourselves to have a chat with God. Honestly, I wasn't used to being still. I was always on the go and hadn't realized how refreshing it could be to just stop and breathe in God's beauty. I really needed to learn to set aside time to talk to God—and to listen. I'm sure at times it was hard for Him to speak to me over the music, phone, TV, and everything else I had plugged in my ears. So, I lay down on the grass and had a little talk with God. I remember asking Him to forgive my attitude and to help me be content even if I weren't with a guy. It felt nice to talk openly and honestly with God—I mean, He knew my heart anyway, right? I hadn't been the happiest lately, but God confirmed that He was working on me and loved me.

I really needed to learn to set aside time to talk to God—and to listen.

One afternoon at the camp, Jason and I were walking back toward the cabins. We both had huge smiles on our faces because we had just braved the ropes course and survived. Carol Ann and Jessica had been too afraid to try it, but Jason and I always shared an adventurous spirit. Part way down the trail, we stumbled across a big tower. I leaned up against the tower for a moment, thinking about how I wasn't dating anyone, and if Jason wanted to kiss me I would let him. *Whoa, what did I just say? What was I thinking?* Jason was my best guy friend. Maybe it was because I'd just gone through a life-or-death experience on the ropes course and suddenly wanted to cling to the other survivor, like in the movies. Who knows? Whatever the reason, I put the thought out of my head. I was *not* going to complicate things between Jason and me. Plus, I needed to get my focus off guys and stop being so boy crazy!

I don't know what it was, but Jason was a bit accident prone around me, especially at camp. While we were playing disc golf, he somehow lost his balance walking across a bridge and ended up in the lake *fully clothed!* Another night, while I was feeling bad and lying on one of the couches, he tried to hug me and ended up accidentally elbowing me in the face instead. Something about when we were together was comical.

Okay, but I have to confess: Jason wasn't the only one with embarrassing moments at camp—mine may have even topped Jason's. There was a zipline that started at the top of a hill and ended in the lake. When it was my turn, I flew down the hill, swung around backward, and ended up hitting the lake with by backside. When I stood up, everyone started pointing and laughing hysterically. Confused, but seeing that they were pointing at my backside, I reached around and touched . . . my cheeks! My shorts were gone! The pressure of the water hitting the back pockets of my blue jean shorts had ripped the pockets down, leaving two large holes. Thank goodness I had my bathing suit on underneath! It was still *really* funny, though, and I decided to keep the shorts as a souvenir of my crazy trip.

Well, like all good things, spring break came to an end, and I said good-bye to camp. It had been packed full of wonderful memories, some scary adventures, good company, and time to refocus on my relationship with God. It was an amazing trip that I would never forget. Unfortunately, it was now time to go back to the real world.

What I Learned

It's hard to find rest when you never stop running.

"Come to Me, all of you who are weary and burdened, and I will give you rest. All of you, take up My yoke and learn from Me, because I am gentle and humble in heart, and you will find rest for yourselves. For My yoke is easy and My burden is light." (Matthew 11:28–30)

Girl Talk

1. I needed a break—from boyfriends, from my phone, from media. What do you need to take a break from so that you can have more time with those who love you, especially God?

_____

_____

_____

_____

2. Okay, if you're jumping from site to site on social networking, while talking on the phone, listening to music, _and_ watching TV, it's going to be pretty much impossible to hear anything else. Do you see any red flags in this lifestyle? If the devil is cunning and smart—which he is—wouldn't keeping you distracted be a great way to make sure you're not talking to God? So how can you make sure Satan doesn't steal your time with God?

_____

_____

_____

_____

3. This may be shocking, but I actually don't like the phrase "quiet time." It makes me think of "time out" and that I'm in trouble. But "quality time" I get. Building a relationship I get. You don't have to be shut up in your room to spend time with God—He is everywhere. Go for a walk, lie down in a field and read the Bible, listen to Christian music, bake, sing . . . whatever you find that you love doing while talking to God. How will you connect with God?

_____

_____

_____

_____

4. Those who obey God are called His friends (John 15:15–16), and we can talk to Him like a friend. He really does hear your prayers (Psalm 34:17). So have you had an honest conversation with God lately? Can you learn to talk to Him like your best friend? Why or why not?

_____

_____

_____

_____

5. It's okay to laugh at ourselves! Now that I've shared one of my most embarrassing moments, what's one of yours?

_____

_____

_____

_____

Chapter 14

Humbled

Even Cinderella's first carriage started out as a pumpkin.

If I had to sum up my junior year in one word, it would be *humbling*. I know I needed it, but that didn't mean I liked it. I kept in touch with Jessica, and Carol Ann and I went to visit her often. Steven and I were on good terms, but it was frustrating to see him with his new girlfriend. I had hopes of winning him back, but his girlfriend was always around to make sure we didn't talk too much. She probably saw through my devious plans. *Argh!*

The toughest time was when prom rolled around. Watching Carol Ann go off with Jessica, Steven, and their friends to the Junior/ Senior while I stayed home wasn't easy. Well, I couldn't invite myself to another school's prom, but I could at least try to find a date to my own. Unfortunately, all my friends had already gotten their dates. And while I was okay not going with a boyfriend, I just wasn't strong enough to go all by myself. So, everyone else got dressed up for the ball while I was left at home, feeling like Cinderella. Okay, so I didn't really have it as bad as Cinderella, but I still wanted to go to the ball. Then I reminded myself of how I got to go last year and my friends didn't. I tried my best to be happy for them, and I actually felt a little better. Jealousy wouldn't have changed anything and would have only made me more miserable. Besides, I was still blessed to be able to hang out with my family who loved me. That may sound like a small thing, but I was about to see that there were people a lot less fortunate.

It was a Wednesday night, and I got home from youth group a few minutes before my mom got home from her church. When she walked through the door, she had a girl with her who didn't look too much older than me. My mom introduced her as Stacy. I politely said hello and smiled, but I was a little puzzled. Was she here to have something to eat? Was she waiting on a ride? I had no clue. Well, I soon found out that she wasn't there to visit at all—my mom had invited her to live with us! Not only that, but she was going to share *my* room!

Honestly, I was shocked! But my mom went on to explain that Stacy was one of two young people at church that night who were stuck in a bad situation. One of the ministers had asked if anyone in the congregation could give these teenagers a place to live. My mom had stepped up. The thing that amazed me most, though, was that my mom was the most unlikely person to offer her home. Let me explain.

I haven't really told you my *full* background. I guess I always wondered if people knew, would they look at me differently? Would they look at me as one of the "less fortunate" (at least by the world's standards)? You see, after the divorce, my mom struggled to make ends meet. Because of her vision problems, she couldn't drive or really work. So my mom, my younger sister, and I all lived in a single-wide on the front row of the trailer park behind Walmart.

Yes . . . I was a trailer park girl. Now do *you* look at me differently? I know it's hard not to stereotype. I remember just a handful of times when someone would make fun of people in trailer parks. Little did they know that was me! Generally, I didn't feel that people treated me differently, but I never gave them a reason to. Just because I didn't have as many material possessions, didn't mean I had to act like I wasn't worth much—though my circumstances could be very humbling at times.

I think our circumstances were part of why my mom asked Stacy to live with us. My mom's humility helped her empathize with others. She wanted to give and didn't worry about gaining anything for herself. She counted on God to provide because she knew she couldn't do it alone. My mom didn't wait for someone else to step up. She didn't make a list of pros and cons and try to work it out financially first. She just said yes because God called her to this selfless act. It's crazy to me to think about all those people in that congregation who had big houses with extra guest rooms and two incomes; yet, God chose to use this most unlikely lady because of her humble heart and willingness to give of all she had. I saw that night that my mom was the kind of person God could use to impact others.

My mom's story reminds me of when Jesus was in the temple and saw a widow give two mites. Others gave much more money than she did, but Jesus said that she had given more than all of them because she had given all that she had (Mark 12:41–44). That's my mom—she gives what she has. Usually it's her time, her prayers, and, if you're lucky, a good home-cooked meal. It's easy to give when you have a lot. It's much harder when you don't know how your own future needs will be met, but that is the kind of heart that is pleasing to God. When you are willing to do what God asks and count on Him completely, He can take the most inadequate people and do the most extraordinary things.

Take David facing Goliath, for example. The whole Israelite army was terrified of Goliath. But David, who was just a teenager, was willing to let God use him in a miraculous way. When I think of that battle, I think of Romans 8:31: "If God is for us, who is against us?" God uses the most unlikely people. He used a teenager. He used my mom. Maybe one day He will use me.

God uses the most unlikely people. . . . Maybe one day He will use me.

Well, in fact, God *did* use me that year . . . and in a way I never expected.

I turned seventeen my junior year. I was actually the oldest of all my friends except for Jason, so, technically I should have already had my driver's license and been driving for a year. Unfortunately, we didn't have money for a car, and I had to have one to take my driving test to get my license. Fortunately, I had lots of friends that I rode around with, but sometimes it seemed like I would never get my license. That was until . . .

One day, while I was at a friend's house, my mom called to tell me the news. *She had bought me a car!* I couldn't believe my ears—and I couldn't wait to get home to see my car. When I arrived, though, I remember just standing and staring at this huge, old, eighties station wagon that was to be my car. It was the kind of car that if someone accidentally hit it, you could just say "that's okay" and go on. For a split second I thought, *This is not at all what I wanted.* However, I quickly shook that thought out of my head. I realized that this was all my mom could give me, and it was really more than she could afford. I decided to suck up my pride and thank her for that big, old station wagon.

Well, this definitely wasn't going to be the car that made the girl, so *I* was going to have to be the girl who made the car. Too many people depend on their stuff to make them happy or popular. My car didn't define who I was—it was just something I owned. If I was going to make it—through school, through life—I was going to have to see that it wasn't the stuff I had that counted. It was what I did with it that made all the difference.

No, my car wasn't shiny or new—it didn't even have automatic windows! But it worked, and I no longer had to worry about hitching a ride. On the contrary, I was getting asked for rides now. It started with one or two people at first, but at some point it turned into a kind of weekly shuttle service to church. There were kids whose parents were too busy to go to church or who just didn't want to—whatever the reason, they didn't have rides to our Wednesday night youth group. So I would check at school and make phone calls each Wednesday to see who needed a ride, then I would make my rounds in the big ole station wagon. What do you know? God really does use the most unlikely people and things!

What I Learned

It's not how much you have that makes you rich; it's a giving and humble heart that God counts as treasure.

The result of humility is fear of the LORD, along with wealth,
honor, and life. (Proverbs 22:4)

Girl Talk

1. Does your stuff make you look good, or do you make your stuff look good? If you didn't have certain things, would you still have the friends you do now? What does that tell you?

_____

_____

_____

_____

2. You know that girl at school that everyone makes fun of because she has a disability, or doesn't know how to fix her hair, or has worn-out clothes—how can you show her love? Isn't she more than what you can see on the outside? Can you stand up to the people making fun of her instead of just laughing along or ignoring it?

_____

_____

_____

_____

3. Jealousy comes pretty easily, but it sure doesn't make you any happier. How do you fight it? What's the opposite of being jealous? (Hint: Read James 3:13–18 to find out.)

_____

_____

_____

_____

4. Isn't it so cool how God can use a young person, a poor person, a not-so-obviously gifted person? He can use us all! It's never about our being *good* enough; it's always about God being *big* enough. Have you given God your talents, your gifts, your passions, and the things you own? You were created to make an impact. Ask God to show you how.

_____

_____

_____

_____

Chapter 15

Oops! I Had It Backward

What's driving your relationship?

I know in my heart it was good for me to not have a boyfriend during this time. It gave me a chance to grow closer to God and to hang out more with my friends—I had felt a little guilty about that. Still, I was glad for this junior year to be over and to have a break from the dating scene around school. It was summer at last and time for a change of pace!

The biggest thing that summer was going to be our Youth Tour. We had been working most of the year to prepare for it. Unfortunately, Jason couldn't go because of the sports he was involved in, but Carol Ann was going and so was Jessica. There were also three other new faces who really stood out—two brothers and a cousin from a neighboring county.

These three guys really made the tour interesting. For one, they were hysterically entertaining in how they interacted with one another. All the girls thought the oldest guy looked like a young George Clooney—plus, he could sing! You can imagine how dreamy-eyed we all were. Oh, and the dreamy-eyed George Clooney went by the name of Chad.

All the girls were talking about Chad and waiting to see which girl he might be interested in. Then I heard from his younger brother that Chad was interested in Carol Ann! I ran to tell her the news—I felt proud that my best friend had beaten out all the other girls. Then, came even more talk . . . Chad's cousin, Seth, was interested in me! I didn't know what to think. I wasn't looking for a relationship and really hadn't talked to Seth that much. What was I going to do?

Well, the rest of the group liked playing matchmaker and begged me to ride on Seth's bus. With everyone pleading for me to give him a chance, I did. I sat in the seat behind Seth so that he could have the chance to talk to me. Seth, however, was really shy, and I had to make the effort for the most part. Seth was nice, but he wasn't really my type. He had a mustache and goatee, and he was thin and dark-haired. It's not that I had my dream guy perfectly drawn out; I just didn't think this was it. But since my other relationships hadn't ended up so great, maybe I needed a new "type." Besides, I had said that I wanted a spiritually mature guy—and that Seth was. He was even the son of a preacher! Maybe I should give this a try.

Well, the rest of the Youth Tour was amazing! God was really teaching us all to be bold in our faith, and we were learning to see Satan's attacks and to pray for one another. Our youth group bonded so much on that trip—especially after the air-conditioning went out on one of the buses. Nothing bonds you like a long road trip on a 90-degree bus! As we pulled into the church parking lot back home, Carol Ann, Chad, Seth, and I agreed that the four of us should go out. Double-dating would be a first for Carol Ann and I, and we were so excited!

This was one of the best times I ever had in dating. Not only was I with a Christian guy who was head-over-heels for me, but at the same time, I didn't have to give up time with my best friend. Our first double-date was bowling. Other times, we would hang out with Chad and Seth's families (who surprisingly all lived within a quarter of a mile of each other). But I have to say, my favorite part was Wednesday nights at youth group. I loved having Seth standing next to me as we praised God together.

School started back up, and even though Seth and I were going to different schools, we saw each other every Wednesday night and almost every weekend. I was totally committed this time to making our long-distance relationship work—and having a car helped. Seth did ask several times if I really liked him, and he seemed worried about the other guys I was around. But Seth had nothing to worry about on my end—I was so in love, and I wasn't about to do anything to mess this up!

This relationship was so incredibly different than my previous ones. I felt so special and respected by Seth as a godly woman. We very rarely kissed, and it was usually just a small kiss good-bye if we did. In the past, I had felt somehow used by other boyfriends who seemed to end up only wanting to make-out rather than just enjoy being with me. I realized that kissing wasn't what made a dating relationship great or even better. It actually seemed to hinder my relationships. I mean, how could I get to know someone better if all we did was kiss? If our lips were occupied, how could we talk? Kissing wasn't quality time. It was wasting time—time that could be used to get to know our likes and dislikes, what we had in common and what was different, and our thoughts for the future, as well as time we could spend with friends and families. Ultimately, kissing was not helping my relationships grow; it was doing just the opposite.

You may have heard the old saying, "Don't put the cart before the horse." It means that you have to put things in the right order so that they'll work properly and you'll be able to move forward. If you put the horse behind the cart, you won't be going anywhere! It's all backward—just as a caboose isn't meant to pull a train. In the same way, if you start off with the physical part of the relationship and don't have anything else to drive your relationship forward, you won't be able to go anywhere. The physical part typically comes easy, but a real relationship takes time and effort.

I think that's why I had been so frustrated in most of my relationships. Not only did I have it backward with the physical part, but I was also blinded. I was kissing frogs—hoping they would eventually turn into my prince—but my head was so clouded by emotions, I couldn't even see that I was kissing a frog! Here's a confession: When I was dating Coleson, I was taken completely by surprise one day when I bumped into his twin brother. I didn't even know he had a brother—let alone a twin! *What else didn't I know about these guys I dated?*

In the movies, relationships always seem to start with a "crush." Merriam-Webster says a *crush* is "an intense and usually passing infatuation." *Infatuation* is then defined as "to inspire with a foolish or extravagant love or admiration." Basically, it's that initial glance at someone you find attractive and the rush of emotions that come with it.

Even though people usually only use the word *crush* when they first meet someone, I think it's often that foolish infatuation that continues, rather than real love. We let our emotions and our ideas of love—or how cute a guy is, or how good he kisses—determine our relationships. Emotions can be so tricky, though, and they sometimes blind you to the truth. If you're counting on that lovey-dovey feeling to be happy, then what will you do when you don't feel it? Just as in life, your relationships will have their ups and downs, and you'll need to be able to make decisions based on more than just romantic feelings.

One of my favorite movies is *Win a Date with Tad Hamilton*. A small-town cashier wins a date with a movie star and is smitten by his good

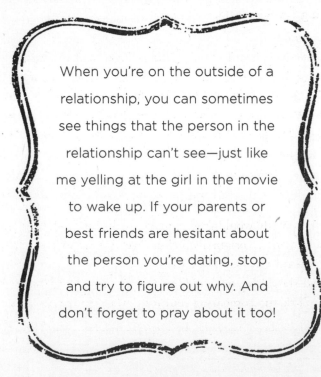

When you're on the outside of a relationship, you can sometimes see things that the person in the relationship can't see—just like me yelling at the girl in the movie to wake up. If your parents or best friends are hesitant about the person you're dating, stop and try to figure out why. And don't forget to pray about it too!

looks and fame. We as the audience know that her best guy friend is the guy who truly loves her and knows her—from her different smiles to what makes her laugh and cry. You just want to yell at her to *"Wake up!"* and see the truth, but she is too blinded by her infatuation with Tad, the movie star.

Before Seth, my best relationship had been with Steven, because it wasn't based on infatuation or kissing. We really enjoyed each other's company and loved to talk. I was starting to see the importance of being friends in a relationship, because when the initial infatuation wears off, you need something more for your relationship to stand on. Honestly, Seth and I weren't as good of friends as Steven and I had been, but for the first time I felt like I had a relationship that put God first.

What I Learned

If you want to be in a relationship that's going somewhere good, you need to move the physical part to the back of your train—otherwise, you're going nowhere good.

Pay careful attention, then, to how you walk—
not as unwise people but as wise—making the most of the time,
because the days are evil. So don't be foolish, but understand
what the Lord's will is. (Ephesians 5:15–17)

Girl Talk

1. Seth honestly wouldn't have made my list of candidates for some-one I would date . . . originally. I think we all tend to make that list of what our dream guy should be like—how tall he should be, what his background should be, his build, his talents, and so on. Make your list and have a little fun comparing your list to your girlfriends' lists.

_____

_____

2. Okay, now look at your list and mark off everything that doesn't have to do with his heart or his character. Do you need to make a new list? Share your new list with your girlfriends. Then read Ephesians 5:25–28 and discuss the qualities you should seek in a godly husband.

_____

_____

_____

_____

3. Speaking of qualities to look for in a spouse . . . this time, write down the qualities you want to have for your future husband, and then discuss those with your friends.

_____

_____

_____

_____

4. So what do you think about the things I said about kissing? How do you view kissing?

_____

_____

_____

_____

5. How can you try to make sure that your relationship with a guy is not just an infatuation?

_____

_____

_____

Chapter 16

With Spring Comes the Rain

Another frog, but still no Prince Charming.

So senior year was looking good . . . *really good!* I possibly had the perfect guy now in Seth, and I was on top of the world.

I was so excited and in love that it spilled over into everything I did. For my project in Industrial Arts class, I even carved a heart out of stone and put Seth's name on one side and mine on the other. I cut it in half, giving him the side with my name and keeping the one with his name for myself. It symbolized that he had a piece of my heart . . . and he did. Okay, yes, maybe a little cheesy, but I didn't care. Carol Ann and I even talked (only partially joking) about having a double wedding. It was kind of crazy to think we talked about marriage, but I guess being a senior led me to thinking about what would come after school. I was definitely happy with Seth and—who knew—he could be *the one*.

One day after school, Carol Ann agreed to come with me to surprise Seth. He was having a tennis tournament, and I thought it could be a cool surprise to show up and support him. We waited for him to arrive at the courts, and when he did, I ran up to hug him. "Surprise!"

I shouted. With a forced smile, he said hello. This wasn't the reaction I had expected, but I tried not to take it too personally. I knew guys were competitive, and maybe I was messing up his focus or made him nervous. So I just said we could catch up after his game. But when the tournament ended, he walked over and said he couldn't really hang out. He had things he needed to do. Okay . . . well . . . . that wasn't cool, and I knew something wasn't right.

We talked on the phone later that night, and Seth finally came clean. He liked another girl. She went to his school, and they had been talking and hanging out. He had decided he was going to date her. So, of course, that meant he was breaking up with me. *Excuse me?* This was the guy who kept asking me if I were being faithful and dedicated to him . . . *and now he was breaking up with me?* I wanted to cry, scream, throw up, and faint from shock—all at the same time. I thought things couldn't have been better in our relationship! We had shared God, friends, church, and family. Now we wouldn't be sharing any of this.

Now, some of you may want to say, "Well, you got payback for how you treated Steven." Maybe. It was a similar situation in ways; yet, I didn't think about that. I couldn't think at all. I was so unbelievably devastated that I felt as if I couldn't even breathe. My chest was caving in, and there was a gaping hole where my heart had been. After the shock and denial came the uncontrollable tears as I curled up in a ball on my bed. I've only ever cried that hard one other time in my life and that was over my parents' divorce. I was completely *crushed*. My happy world had fallen apart, and there was absolutely nothing I could do about it. Seth had made his choice, and it wasn't me.

Even I was surprised by how hard I took this break-up. I know we were only dating, but I had trusted Seth completely with my heart. I had trusted that this good Christian guy would take care of me and love me. I expected more from him than any other boyfriend, and he let me down. I had gotten so high on the happiness of our relationship that I took a very big fall.

I really wasn't able to function like myself anymore. I saw people around me who were happy, and I wanted to at least pretend to be happy for them, but I couldn't seem to find the strength. The hardest thing was that Carol Ann was still dating Seth's cousin, and it was a constant reminder of what I no longer had.

Church was no longer as happy a place for me either. I would imagine Seth and me standing there, singing together, but he was no longer there. I would sometimes leave church service crying. I had also gotten close to his family, but I would no longer be able to see them either. Then to top off all the awfulness, I realized I wouldn't have Seth as my date for Senior Prom.

Everyone tried their best to comfort me. Jason offered his condolences by offering to date me . . . as always. Carol Ann was a good listener and promised to give that other girl the "evil eye" if she ever saw her. (Carol Ann could

The Lord your God is with you wherever you go.
—Joshua 1:9

seriously stare people down until they were afraid!) But nothing really comforted me until, one day, my mom taped something to my mirror. It was a card she had special ordered with my name and a Bible verse on it. First of all, it is rare for me to have anything with my name on it since my name was made up by my mom and very unique. Under my name it said "Blessed." The Bible verse was Joshua 1:9: "Haven't I commanded you: be strong and courageous? Do not be afraid or discouraged, for the Lord your God is with you wherever you go." I cried. This time, though, it was a cry of relief. Had I forgotten that God was still there and loved me? That He could carry me through anything and give me the strength I needed? I cherished the card my mom gave me and read it often. I was blessed. I knew then I could get through this.

What I Learned

God *never* leaves me; rather, it's I who tend to stray away.

❧

*Haven't I commanded you: be strong and courageous? Do not
be afraid or discouraged, for the LORD your God is with you
wherever you go. (Joshua 1:9)*

Girl Talk

1. Have you ever had your heart broken like I did, whether by a
guy, a friend, or even family? Have you reached out to God to give you
strength to forgive and move on? Read Matthew 18:21–22 and Ephesians
4:32. Ask God to help you forgive those who have hurt you.

_____

_____

_____

_____

2. Seth broke my heart, but God never will. My heart is safe with
God and so is yours. Check out His promises in Psalm 73:26 and Psalm
34:18. What do they tell you about how God cares for the brokenhearted?

_____

_____

_____

3. God says we have to endure trials, but He also gives us hope. Do
you trust Him with your future? Take a look at a few of my favorite Bible
verses: Proverbs 3:5, John 16:33, 2 Corinthians 4:8–18, Jeremiah 29:11, and
Romans 8:28. What do these verses say to you about trusting God?

_____

_____

_____

_____

4. Do you believe a broken heart can be God's path to something much greater?

_____

_____

_____

_____

5. It's okay to mourn, but *only* for a time. List some ways you can get out from under your self-pity. (For example: Tell God "thank You" for as many things as you can possibly list. It's hard to be sad when you're being thankful.) What about the music you listen to? People you're getting advice from?

_____

_____

_____

_____

Chapter 17

Imperfect World, Imperfect People

Since nobody's perfect, it's a good thing God is!

❧❧❧❧❧❧❧❧❧❧❧❧

Even though I had God to pull me through the break-up with Seth, that didn't mean I wasn't still hurting. I'd had high expectations for Seth—more so than the other guys I dated—mostly because he seemed to be such a great Christian guy. So how could this Christian guy hurt me so badly? After I had calmed down a little bit, I realized that, *duh,* Seth wasn't perfect. Being a Christian doesn't make anyone perfect or even better than anyone else. It just means we have a relationship with Jesus who forgives our sins and imperfections and helps us be more like Him.

My problem, though, had been much deeper than just my fallen expectations of Seth. I didn't realize it at the time, but I had let Seth become the center of my world—and I was the one who put him there. I put him at the center of everything I loved most . . . God, friends, and family. Think about it: I started enjoying church, no longer just because of my time with God, but because Seth was there with me. I loved hanging out with Carol Ann because we could double-date. I loved being a part of family events with Seth, because I felt special and part of this beautiful family picture. So when Seth was stripped away, all those aspects of my life were left lacking. Why? Because no guy is meant to be the center of your world or the center of your heart.

Super-hard lesson to learn . . . and I was only *beginning* to learn it. I mean, I had been the best girlfriend I could possibly be! Yet, it still wasn't enough. *I* couldn't be enough. No person can be enough. An imperfect girl joined with an imperfect guy *cannot* have a perfect relationship. So then how do you have a good relationship? Well, God was still working to show me how.

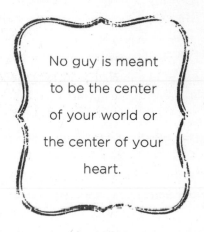

No guy is meant to be the center of your world or the center of your heart.

While I was trying to figure out why my own world had fallen apart, I got the news that a friend at school had died in a car accident. The phone call left me completely numb. This was the first time I was faced with a person's mortality and the thought of life after death. And this was first time I had lost someone I really knew. I didn't know how to deal with it, and I didn't know what to think of it except—*Why? What was wrong with this world?*

We all want our lives to be perfect, right? A perfect relationship, perfect friends, perfect family, perfect job, perfect place to live, and on and on. Well, I have good and bad news about that. First, the bad—life will never be perfect—not on this earth. Nothing is perfect in this world— not people, places, or things. Oh, once it was—in the Garden of Eden. And ever since then, we humans have had this longing for that perfect place and perfect relationship with God. But we can't be completely ful- filled by this world.

Yes, the day is coming when we, as believers in Jesus, will have a per- fect paradise once again. But what do we do until then? That's the good news! There is a way to fill that longing in our heart to be perfectly loved and to know that our life matters. It all comes down to God. We have a God-shaped hole inside of us that only He can fill. We may try to fill it with other things or with other relationships, but ultimately only God will do. I had given Seth my heart, and he had left it broken. But when I gave my heart back to God, I was overcome with peace and joy. I could trust God completely with my heart because He *is* perfect and promises to *never* leave me—no matter how imperfect I am.

And one more thing, this imperfect world is not our home. God says we're like foreigners living in another land. So when I feel like I don't fit in or life seems unfair or unjust, I can know this is only temporary. I am really a princess disguised as a normal girl, and I actually belong in the palace with my King. Not because I did anything to deserve it—oh no—but because Jesus laid down His life to purchase a place in paradise for me. So when the tough days come, I can whisper, "This world is not my home. The best is yet to come."

Just because Christians are foreigners in this world, doesn't mean we just sit back and wait for the world to end, though. Of course not! God wants us to have a fulfilling life no matter where He has us right

"For I know the plans I have for you"—this is the LORD's declaration—"plans for your welfare, not for disaster, to give you a future and a hope."—Jeremiah 29:11

now—whether it's being single, in a broken family, at a new school, or in a tough job. God doesn't promise that a life following Him will be easy. This world was cruel to His own Son, so we shouldn't expect any different.

What's amazing is how God uses both the good and the bad. Jesus' disciples had amazing days with thousands being saved, people being healed, and food being multiplied for everyone to eat. Then, there were days of being run out of town, beaten, thrown into prison, and, yes, even news of their friend's death. But God used both their good days and their bad to show the people His love and power. Stephen's death (Acts 6–7) pushed Christians to run and scatter for fear of losing their lives. But God used this awful event to take the good news of Jesus to other parts of the world. God even used Paul's time in prison to witness to a guard and lead his whole family to believe in Jesus. Yep, God will use your life too—the good and the bad—to impact the world . . . if you let Him.

Once I broke free from my pit of despair, God revealed a truth to me about myself. God showed me that I always ran to Him, pleading for help when I was having a hard time or bad day. Yet, I didn't run to Him or pray to Him nearly as much when things were going great. So I got out a piece of paper and my watercolor pencils. I drew a beach with a beautiful sunset going into the water, a palm tree, and birds flying in the sky. Then on it I wrote: "Dechari—be as close to God in the good times as the bad, and He will see you through both." I hung it on my mirror as a constant reminder that I was going to have the bad with the good, but I could always count on God to see me through it all.

What I Learned

Don't let the imperfectness of this world get you down, because this world wasn't meant to fill your soul . . . only God makes you whole.

*Therefore we do not give up. Even though our
outer person is being destroyed, our inner person
is being renewed day by day. For our momentary light
affliction is producing for us an absolutely incomparable
eternal weight of glory. So we do not focus on what is seen,
but on what is unseen. For what is seen is temporary,
but what is unseen is eternal. (2 Corinthians 4:16–18)*

Girl Talk

1. What is the center of your world right now? Is it God? Or is it a boy, a friend, a hobby? If God isn't the One holding your heart and holding you together, then how will you handle the difficult times in life?

_____

_____

_____

_____

2. Why are we, as girls, so quick to give our heart away? Are there ways you can better protect your heart? (Take a look at Proverbs 4:23.)

_____

_____

_____

_____

3. Do you ever feel dissatisfied with your life? Might it be that closeness with God that you are missing?

_____

_____

_____

_____

4. In looking at Jesus and His disciples' time here on earth—both the amazing days and the difficult ones—what new perspectives do you have about your time here? What do you think about this world not being your real home? Does it excite you, scare you, or make you happy or sad?

---

5. Read James 1:17. Don't forget about God when things are going great; instead, give God the credit and thanks for the blessings in your life. What are a couple of your favorite memories or moments that you are thankful for?

Chapter 18

Finish Strong: Senior Year

When one adventure ends, another begins.

❦❦❦❦❦❦❦❦❦❦❦❦❦

I had been waiting for my senior year for so long, but now that it was here, I had a lot of mixed emotions. At first, I couldn't wait for it to be over, but then as the time drew nearer, I wasn't sure I wanted it to end. I had some good—no, some *fantastic*—memories! It all started my freshman year with an extended group of friends, going to youth rallies, Jason and Kristy getting saved, joining a dynamic youth group, being mentored by college students who loved Jesus, witnessing our faith on tours, learning responsibility, being adventurous, surviving embarrassing moments, being humbled, and learning to heal from broken hearts. There were dresses and dances, halls full of fun conversations, notes passed in class, crazy projects I stayed up all night to finish, relationships I grew from, and friendships that would last forever. Why had I ever wished for it to go by any faster? High school was a roller coaster, but it made me a lot of who I am—and who God was molding me to be. I was going to treasure these last moments I had. And no matter how the year had begun, I was hoping for a great ending. And why wouldn't it be great? It was my *senior year!!!*

Though my heartache over Seth was still looming, I did have a lot of other things to take my mind off it. First, I had some big senior projects to focus on. The kind where if you failed, you wouldn't graduate!

I also moved up in the work world. Yep, from grocery store cashier to retail cashier at the Walmart right next to my house. I enjoyed the interaction with people. Plus, our town was small, so if you wanted to bump into anyone, Walmart was the happening place.

I still had "the wagon" and was still driving people to church. There were youth rallies, cool Christian concerts, church basketball games, and tons of baseball games after school. Jason was the lead pitcher. I usually laid out a blanket behind home plate to watch the game, so he could always see me cheering him on. Okay, so I was sometimes working on my tan, but I was still watching . . . for the most part. Even our church had a softball league, and Kristy, Carol Ann, and I tried to make it to every game. Now that I think about it, when did I ever work?

Yep, I was staying busy. I didn't really even have time for a boyfriend anymore, which was probably for the best. Knowing me, I would have made my future decisions based on a guy over anything else. *That* would have been scary. All my friends were putting in college applications. Jason wanted to be a baseball player for Appalachian State, which was the university in our hometown. Carol Ann wanted to go to Appalachian too. Kristy was off to Wilmington, and Jessica was applying for Asbury. But me? I had no plans. This is where Carol Ann stepped in with a little push. She said I should at least apply somewhere so that I had the option. So I filled out my application to Appalachian, and . . . I was accepted!

It was both scary and exciting as I prepared to take this next big step into the unknown world of college. Was I ready for this? I had only seen TV shows and movies about college life, and it looked crazy. So how would this Christian girl make it in the college world?

I wrote this poem for my dad who supported me in everything I set my mind to. It seemed very fitting for what I was going through my senior year. It's about a young girl who realizes she has to grow up, but also knows she will always need both her father and her heavenly Father as she learns to live out the Fruits of the Spirit.

My Little Girl

How wonderful it is being a little girl
with ponytails, frills, and not a care in the world.

Can't I stay a little girl and just always have fun,
with endless days of toys, running, and playing in the sun?

Must I go off to school and be all alone?
Do I have to make choices all on my own?

What if I mess up? What if I fall?
"Well, my little girl, with **Patience** *you will grow tall."*

What do I do when my circumstances get too tough?
"You'll have to grow in **Faith** *and know you'll have enough."*

The world can seem so cruel. It may be hard to keep up the
fight.
"That's why you'll grow in **Goodness** *and show them some
light."*

What if the world tries to influence me in the wrong way?
"You will have to be able to use **Self-Control** *each and every
day."*

What if people are mean and begin to make fun?
"You will learn to **Love** *through the love of God's Son."*

So many choices—what if it's only my desires I'm trying to fill?
"By growing in **Meekness***, you will learn to follow God's perfect
will."*

Will I be like the people who moan, complain, and always seem
sad?
"No. As you learn to ask for **Joy***, in everything you can be glad."*

So how should I show my faith and let people see who I really
am?
"With the boldness of a lion, but most of all the **Gentleness** *of
a lamb."*

So growing up shouldn't be too hard, because I have a Dad like
you.
"At times it will be tough, but learn to receive God's **Peace** *and
He will see you through."*

> *"Remember, with every step I will hold your hand and
> be by your side until you can walk well on your own.
> Even then I will not leave you, because to me
> you are still my little girl, even though you have grown."*
> —from Galatians 5:22–23

Well, I finished my senior year strong with good grades, good relationships, a good outlook on life, and a hope for the future. I even got to
go to my senior prom. (I asked Coleson to go, purely as a friend.) It was
nice to get dressed up one last time. I had asked Jason to save me a dance
. . . but you know he never did. So I playfully scolded him and said he
still owed me that dance.

At last, it was graduation day. Light blue caps and gowns filled the
auditorium. Name after name was called. When finally it was my turn
to walk across the stage, I couldn't help but smile. I had done it! We had
done it! Caps flew through the air in celebration. Four years were coming
to a close and a new chapter in our lives was about to start.

What I Learned

Don't sell yourself short. Give it all you have, and then give God all
the glory for what He does with it.

I have fought the good fight, I have finished the race, I have kept
the faith. There is reserved for me in the future the crown of
righteousness, which the Lord, the righteous Judge, will give me
on that day, and not only to me, but to all those who have loved
His appearing. (2 Timothy 4:7–8)

Girl Talk

1. Read Ecclesiastes 3:1–13. For everything there is a season. High
school was definitely a season for me! What season are you going
through right now? What is God teaching you in it? Does knowing that
this is only a season give you hope for the future?

_____

_____

_____

_____

2. Read 1 Corinthians 9:24–27. Paul compares life to running a race. What does it take to be a good, long-distance runner? How would this race analogy apply to the things you need to be doing in your life? Paul talks about two different types of rewards—earthly and heavenly. What might these be?

_____

_____

_____

_____

3. A wise person seeks to learn (Proverbs 18:15). Unfortunately, I didn't realize how much of a gift a free education was until I was out of high school. How do you view your education?

_____

_____

_____

_____

4. Read James 1:5 and Psalm 25:4–10. Have you asked God's guidance in that next step in your life? Where to go? What classes to take?

_____

_____

_____

_____

5. How do you want to finish strong this year?

_____

_____

_____

_____

Chapter 19

New Girl on Campus

Just because you can, doesn't mean you should.

Even though I had graduated, not all of my high school traditions came to an end. There was still a Youth Tour that summer before college . . . and it had the potential to be the best one yet. My younger sister, Brittany, was finally old enough to come with us this year. Carol Ann was there, of course, and Kristy, as well as some other great friends from church. Carol Ann's boyfriend, Chad, came on tour again, but thankfully Seth did not.

We were going to do a production called *The Army of God,* and I was surprised when I was asked to play the main part. I felt kind of inadequate, but honored at the same time. I would give it my best and try to play the part from my heart. As I learned the role, I saw that it really wasn't so far off from my actual life. It was about a teenage girl in search of really knowing God. As she learns about His love and begins to share Him with her lost friends, she comes to see that she's on a battlefield as a warrior for Christ.

I guess I was hoping that God would somehow use me in big ways in this role, despite the fact that I didn't feel very talented. It just meant I had to lean on God that much more to play the part like I should. By the end of the tour, though, I wasn't really acting. At one point in the program, I was supposed to pray for my friends' protection against Satan's lies—and I was truly praying out loud for my friends. It was awesome!

You see, we weren't just *acting out* how Satan tries to tempt us, destroy us, and ultimately keep us from God—we were living it on this tour. There were arguments, people getting hurt, troubles with our van, and more. We were doing something to stand up for God and spread the good news of Jesus, which meant we were declaring battle against Satan—and Satan was fighting back. He wanted God's army divided and feeling defeated, but we were learning to be on guard for the attacks.

Put on the full armor of God so that you can stand against the tactics of the Devil.
—Ephesians 6:11

Instead of running off, getting upset, or fighting with each other, our leaders taught us to fight Satan on our knees in prayer. We were in a spiritual battle, and we needed to put on our armor (Ephesians 6:10–20) and be ready to fight!

Though the tour had been a battlefield, it was still terrific because God taught me to lean on Him for the victory. That's what I needed to know before I took this next step into college. College would be its own battlefield of living for God versus letting Satan have a heyday with my life. There is so much freedom in college—to enjoy, to experiment with, or to abuse. It's a time when faith can either grow stronger or be abandoned all together.

When college time came, it brought lots of changes, though a few things stayed the same. I decided to live at home, since campus was only a few miles away. (*And* I would have home-cooked meals and someone to do my laundry!) The downside of living off campus was that I had to worry about parking, which was outrageously expensive and practically nonexistent. Parking passes *started* at $500. That wasn't even an option for my piggy bank. Option "B" was the handful of free parking spots on the edge of campus. If you were brave enough and had the patience, you could swarm around them with all the other vultures ready to swoop in for a spot. Luckily for me, though, I had an option "C"—Jason. Jason's family got a rental house over the summer, right across the street from campus. He offered to let me park there and then walk to class from his house. I definitely took him up on it! We started timing our walks in the mornings so that we could walk together. Then, depending on our schedules, we would sometimes catch up in the afternoons. It was so much more fun walking with a friend, especially on a big, new campus.

I was still working at Walmart, but I had moved from just cashiering to also greeting. Actually, I volunteered for the job. No one else seemed to like greeting people and giving out smiley face stickers, but I did. So I was nineteen and greeting people at Walmart when, one day, this lady walks up to me, talking a million miles an hour. She and her husband had seen me working and wanted to hire me to work at their car dealership. I didn't think much about it at first. All I knew was that this lady was interrupting my smiley face duties! Once I let it sink in, though, I thought, *What's the harm in checking it out?*

It was my first actual job interview—before I'd just turned in applications. Well, they offered me the job and more money. They seemed really nice, so I accepted. I was a part-time receptionist/cashier/filing clerk/customer service representative. It was the most responsibility I'd had so far. With a little patience and some needed critiques, I turned into their 5-Star Customer Service Manager. It ended up being the best job I probably ever had, mainly because of the great Christian couple I worked for, Mike and Mary.

As I'd expected, college did offer a lot of freedom—and lots of decisions to make. Which class? Which club? Which activity? There were so many cool activities to choose from. On the other hand, there were also a lot of not-so-cool activities—like drinking. It didn't matter if students were of legal age or not, drinking seemed to be "the thing" to try. People didn't even stop to think if they should drink; they just did it because they could. Sounds like that same lie Satan fed Eve: *"Look! God's keeping something good from you."* Sure, it was made out to be fun, but all you had to do was look at the consequences to see that it was just the opposite. Drinking led to numbing your senses, making poor decisions, ignoring your problems, keeping you from real relationships, and endangering lives. It created dependency, addiction, and sometimes anger and violence. My sweet boss, Mary, broke into tears in the office one day as she told me how alcohol was completely destroying her son's life. Anything there is a rehabilitation center for should be your first clue that it's probably not something good for your life.

I was so thankful that I didn't go down that road. I credit God and my good friends who kept me accountable—and also, I knew how much fun I could have without alcohol. And fun I had! One of the best things Carol Ann, Jason, and I did was try out some dance classes. These weren't the swaying back and forth to slow songs and grinding to fast ones (yuck). Nope, these required actual moves and skills. I was totally hooked! Everyone's favorite was the Swing Dance Club. You know—the oldies type dancing you may have seen in movies. Come to find out Jason had some pretty great rhythm! Better than me for sure. So I finally got my dance with Jason as he ended up being my dance partner. And we tried all the crazy moves—flips, aerials, and all kinds of fancy tricks. Swing dancing became a weekly routine for a bunch of us. It was great exercise, very social, and a ton of fun.

Yes, college was different, but I had a feeling I was going to like it. Then, one day, as I was walking across campus, I spotted Jason in the distance, heading off to class. I paused and smiled with a bit of a question mark on my face. Did Jason look different somehow? Huh, I guess he actually looked like a college guy. Definitely different than that geeky little love-struck boy I had met my freshman year of high school. We were all growing up, I guess. For some reason it left me with a happy thought. I sure wasn't the same girl I was that freshman year of high school. I wasn't sure who I was just yet, but one thing was certain . . . I was the new girl on campus.

What I Learned

Since God says that most people are on a path to destruction—why follow them there? Don't be afraid to show them there's another way!

❧

Enter through the narrow gate. For the gate is wide and the road is broad that leads to destruction, and there are many who go through it. How narrow is the gate and difficult the road that leads to life, and few find it. (Matthew 7:13–14)

Girl Talk

1. I heard a pastor once say, "Does your life require a gospel explanation?" What he meant was, do you live in such a way that people wonder why you're different and the only answer is Jesus?

_____

_____

_____

2. Read Ephesians 6:10–20. What stands out to you when you read about the armor of God? Try praying this over yourself first thing in the morning. Ask a parent or friend to pray it with you.

_____

_____

_____

3. Would you handle things differently and with greater wisdom if you were more aware of the spiritual battle? For example, if someone is being cruel to you, take a step back. Could he or she be hurting and

taking it out on you? Might Satan be attacking the relationship? Does the person even know God? Now—how will you start fighting your battles?

_____

_____

_____

_____

4. Just because you can do something, doesn't mean you should. Read Ecclesiastes 10:1–3. How can you tell if you're the fool? How can you keep your heart going in the right direction?

_____

_____

_____

_____

Chapter 20

Freshman on Fire

Before you enter the dragon's lair, be sure to put your armor on.

Well, all the extracurricular activities were fun, but now it was time to hit the books. My classes were pretty much the basics everyone was required to take . . . math, biology, history, English. So here we go with the 101s. Everyone has their strong and weak subjects. Math and English, I did pretty well in, but biology kicked my booty. I worked my tail off with a study group and got a "C"—for which I was very thankful! Then there was history, which typically I found very boring. But *this* history class was going to be anything but boring.

History 101, Day One: Carol Ann, another friend named Allison, and I had planned our schedule to share this class. As class started, we, of course, sat next to each other. The teacher—we'll call her Ms. Walls—started off class with a series of questions to the class.

"Who in here believes that God created the heavens and the earth?"

I was a bit surprised by the question. High school had abided by the notion of "separation of church and state," so religion was never talked about in class. Maybe college was different, I thought. So I, along with my two friends, raised our hands.

"Who believes in the virgin birth?"

"Who believes Jesus is the Son of God?"

We kept raising our hands and started nodding our heads like "Yeah . . . we believe in all that." Ms. Walls continued with other questions on biblical foundations. Hey, now this was my kind of history class! Then, just as I was getting really excited, Ms. Walls' face quickly transformed from kind and questioning to glaring and condemning. *It was a trap!* She went on to say what kind of stupid, awful people we were if we believed in those things. I couldn't even comprehend all the specifics of what she was saying. All I could think as she yelled at us was, "Is this really happening?"

After class was over, the three of us picked our jaws up off the floor and walked out of the room in shock. Ms. Walls wasn't out to encourage the Christians in class; she was out to target us! And this was just History 101! How did I get in so deep? From day one, we knew that we each had a bull's-eye on our forehead.

I'd had people not accept my faith before or not want to hear about Jesus, but I'd never had anyone actually attack it like that. Especially a public attack from an adult with such vengeance. It was quite scary and surreal. I had known that college could test my faith, but I hadn't known what that would really look like. Now I knew. I told my mom what happened. Her response was, "Well, it sounds like the three of you are going through the fire . . . just like Shadrach, Meshach, and Abednego did."

I think my mom may be a genius. I could totally relate to Shadrach, Meshach, and Abednego! They were young men, away from home in a new land. They had been forced to serve the king, and God gave them favor in his sight. The king, though, believed in other false gods and not the true God. (Yep, got that—a new place with people who didn't believe in God. *Check.*) One day, the king had a statue of himself made and ordered everyone to either bow down to it or be thrown into a fiery furnace. Shadrach, Meshach, and Abednego refused. Well, the king was furious, but he gave them one more chance because he liked them. Maybe he thought, *Okay, you're new at this, but this is how we do things around here.* (Pressure to follow the crowd. *Check.*) But this was their response:

> If the God we serve exists,
> then He can rescue us from the
> furnace of blazing fire, and He can
> rescue us from the power of you,
> the king. But even if He does not
> rescue us, we want you as king to
> know that we will not serve your
> gods or worship the gold statue
> you set up. —Daniel 3:17–18

Well, into the furnace they went. It was so hot that even the guards putting them in died. Then a miracle happened. The king was astonished to see not three men in the furnace, but four! And they were all walking around unharmed. When the king let them out, they didn't even smell like smoke. God had protected them in that fire, and they came out unharmed. The king then knew that their God was real. There's no doubt in my mind that God put those three guys in that situation so that He could be made known to the king and the people. Shadrach, Meshach, and Abednego went through the fire, and God came out shining.

Don't you think that God had Carol Ann, Allison, and me in that class to show His love and light to Ms. Walls? Maybe even the whole class? While she didn't have an actual fire to throw us in—though if it were legal she might have—Ms. Walls was out to test our faith. We could have run away by asking for another class, but there was something about the three of us together that made it easier to stand strong. And it wasn't just the three of us, anyway. There was a fourth. God was right there with us, and He would see us through.

I think of Jesus and how He was made fun of, yelled at, and then ultimately tortured and killed in the most brutal and embarrassing way. He didn't go through all that for His benefit. No, He did it purely for yours and mine! He could have stepped away at any time and said this isn't worth it, but He didn't. He knew you and I were totally worth it. Jesus said, "Whoever denies Me before men, I will also deny him before My Father in heaven" (Matthew 10:33). Jesus stood strong to save me, and there's no way I could deny Him.

Jesus also told us how to get through the name-calling and attacks, and how to treat our enemies. He said to love them and pray for them (Matthew 5:44–47)! Not our normal reaction, I know. Jesus said it's easy to love people who like you and treat you well, but *God's* love is loving even those who do you wrong. Think about it: if someone treats you wrong and you repay them with kindness, what a statement for God that makes! People will question why you're different.

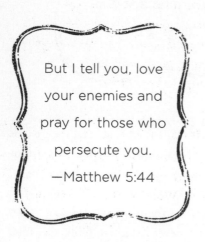

But I tell you, love your enemies and pray for those who persecute you.
—Matthew 5:44

I'm not saying it's easy. It's actually going against your very nature. You want to fight back, to repay hateful words with more hateful words. Don't let others defeat you. Their cruelty isn't really about what they have against you; it's about what they lack inside. If they lack Jesus in their life, how can we expect them to be like Him? I don't know what made Ms. Walls hate Christians so much. Perhaps someone in her past hurt her. Whatever it was, I knew she didn't know the God I knew—the One whose love is so amazing it can't help but spill out to others. So maybe we could show her His love.

That we did. We prayed for her salvation while killing her with kindness. As time went by, her hardened heart toward Christians seemed to be cracking. Her condemning demeanor softened. We actually began having conversations outside of just schoolwork. I think she was surprised to see us go out of our way to say hello and ask her how her day was. We never saw Ms. Walls come to know Jesus as her Savior, but we left the class unharmed by the fire she put us through, and I think Jesus' love was shown because of it.

What I Learned

You'll never walk through the fire alone as long as you know the One True God.

You rejoice in this, though now for a short time you
have had to struggle in various trials so that the genuineness
of your faith—more valuable than gold, which perishes though
refined by fire—may result in praise, glory, and honor at the
revelation of Jesus Christ. (1 Peter 1:6–7)

Girl Talk

1. Your faith is going to be tested. Are you willing to go through the fire if it means God will come out shining more brightly? Or will you hide your faith to avoid being persecuted? What are you so afraid of?

_____

_____

_____

_____

2. Sometimes people who don't know God only want to see you fall. They want to see that your faith is not real so that they can justify not following God. For example, have you seen people go after those who publicly say they're waiting until marriage to have sex? My pastor says, "When others are doing wrong, I will stand strong." How can we help each other stand strong?

_____

_____

_____

_____

3. God has put you where you are to show Jesus to those around you. So where are you right now? Make a list of those you need to pray for and "kill with kindness." Share your list with your friends and pray for those on their lists too.

_____

_____

_____

4. It's easy to hang out with and love on people who are like us. But Jesus hung out with the unpopular, and He loved the unlovable. He even told us to pray for our enemies. Why?

_____

_____

_____

_____

5. There will be times when you'll have to enter some dangerous territory. How can you best be prepared to fight the enemy who's ready to tear you to shreds?

_____

_____

_____

Chapter 21

A Different Kind of Girl

Mirror, mirror, when you look at me . . . what kind of girl do you see?

Now the business owners I worked for, Mike and Mary, had a son named Brandon, who hung out at the dealership a lot in the afternoons. He was at least one to two years older than me. He was tall with blond hair, a deep voice, and was pretty well-built, I guess you could say. Believe it or not, though, I was actually not boy crazy at this moment in time. I had cooled things down from high school, and my focus was on doing well at my new job. However, Brandon caught me a couple of times when I was leaving work and asked if I'd like to go out sometime. Each time I said thank you, but no. I didn't really know him, plus he was my bosses' son. That just seemed too weird.

But Brandon kept asking. Being the people pleaser I was, combined with my *slight* weakness for guys, I finally said okay. What could it hurt to hang out one time? And I was sure it would only be one time. You see, Brandon was kind of a "bad boy" and a partier. I even wondered why he'd want to be around a person like me. I didn't drink. I didn't have sex. I didn't party—at least not the kind he probably did. I figured Brandon just didn't really know me. Well, he was about to see I was a different kind of girl. My plan was to go out with him once, let him figure out that I'm not his type, and then he'd leave me alone.

Well, Brandon picked me up, and I honestly don't remember much about the beginning of the date. The part that vividly stands out is when Brandon took me back to his parents' (and my bosses'!) house. *Oh,* he was still living at home! I hadn't realized that and therefore hadn't thought this part through. Mike and Mary definitely didn't know I was going out with Brandon that night. I'm pretty sure they were quite surprised to see me, but were very gracious. Still, I think I turned two shades redder when I said hello.

Brandon and I chatted as he showed me around the house. As we made our way downstairs, he stopped in a room where it was just the two of us and took a seat on the couch. He invited me to sit with him to talk. *Yeah, right.* I knew where this kind of atmosphere led, and I saw how Brandon was looking at me. Time to put "Operation Good Girl" into motion. I sat down, turned to Brandon, and quickly blurted out, "I think there are some things that you should know about me. Just so you know . . . I *don't* drink, I *don't* do drugs, I *don't* party, and I am waiting until I get married before I have sex."

There, I said it. I dropped the bomb and waited for the date to explode. There was a moment of silence as I waited for him say, "Well, it was nice meeting you" and then take me home. But he didn't. I may have shocked him a little with my honesty and forwardness, but he seemed kind of pleased. Now *I* was shocked. He said okay, and we continued on with a casual conversation without the pressure of him making any moves on me.

Surprisingly, Brandon and I continued to hang out now and again after that night. We weren't really boyfriend and girlfriend. It was a kind of casual dating, I guess. Deep down, I think we both knew that we weren't truly compatible. Yet, I was intrigued by the way he reacted to my "bombshell," and he was intrigued by the fact that I said it.

Maybe Brandon had done some not so great things in his life, but he was a gentleman when I was around. A tall, handsome, gentleman with muscles. Most of all, he seemed to really respect me. The interesting dynamics of our "relationship" continued throughout my freshman year. But no matter how he acted around me, I could sense he wasn't fully ready to give up the secret lifestyle he kept hidden from me. It wasn't up to me to change him, though. I couldn't anyway—I had learned that from Evan. God had to be the One to change Brandon's heart and lifestyle, so that meant I couldn't really let myself get too close. However, it was cool how God used our relationship to open both our eyes. Before Brandon, I figured the cool, good-looking, popular guys only liked girls who were mysterious, promiscuous, and partiers—like the girls in the movies. And I think Brandon learned that those weren't the only kind of girls to choose from. Man, had we both been sold a lie!

Later, Mary (Brandon's mom) told me that I had totally changed Brandon's outlook on women. She explained that he had never met anyone like me before—someone who had values and beliefs and was willing to stick to them. That you can be a "good girl" and still be cool, sweet, and fun. He had mostly met girls who tried to be what they thought he wanted and who compromised themselves to get affection. Mary said Brandon started looking for a different type of woman—one more like me. Wow! I never thought I could make that kind of an impact. It was so encouraging to know that the world's view of how a woman should be in a relationship was wrong. Guys do want a good girl!

You can be a "good girl" and still be cool, sweet, and fun.

So why is Hollywood selling us this cheap version of what we and our relationships should look like? More important, *Why are we buying it?* Why are we settling for a knock-off when we can have the real thing? Check out the Proverbs 31 description of a woman. Where is she in the media? All I see is a cookie-cutter mold of what we are told we should be—slender (even to the point of being unhealthy), tall, big busted, sexy, a little provocative to lure in the men, somewhat of a tease, a bit wild even if that means doing illegal or dangerous things . . . oh, and don't forget the flawless, airbrushed skin! A woman's worth in the media is mostly based on her looks and sexuality. Thankfully, God calls us to be *much more* than that!

God calls us to be a different kind of girl. He doesn't want us to be imitators of the world, but imitators of Christ (Ephesians 5:1–5). Don't sell yourself short and become a knock-off version of who you really are. Be the real deal—the girl God created you to be! That's what Brandon saw in me. I didn't compromise my morals to get attention. I didn't try to be with the in-crowd by drinking. I definitely wasn't a perfect representation by any means, but He did get to see Christ in me. I think that's what truly made me beautiful to him—my heart for following Jesus.

I was so happy to know that who I was in Christ was what mattered most, and that I didn't have to change that to get a guy. I knew not everyone would appreciate my morals like Brandon did, but I had learned that most guys do want a good girl—whether they realize it yet or not. I was still on my search for the real deal—and I knew I wasn't going to settle for the Hollywood version of a relationship. I knew I wanted more—and the first step to getting it was to be that girl who wasn't afraid to be different.

What I Learned

A woman of high morals is a rare find. So be that diamond that shines in a rough world, for you will be treasured.

Who can find a capable [virtuous] wife?
She is far more precious than jewels. (Proverbs 31:10)

Girl Talk

1. Were you thinking the same thing I was? That as soon as I listed all the things I wasn't going to do, that the good-looking guy would run the other way. But he didn't. What do you think about that? What would that say about the guy if he did run the other way?

_____

_____

_____

_____

2. Which guy do you want to be with—the one who respects and cherishes your God-given standards *or* the one who wants you to compromise them? What about your friends? Are you hanging out with people who only like you when you're following the crowd, *or* are you hanging out with friends who like you for who you are and encourage you to stay strong in your faith?

_____

_____

_____

3. So why do you think being the "good girl" is so often made out to be a bad thing?

_____

_____

_____

4. Read Proverbs 31:10–31. Using your own words, what characteristics stand out to you about this type of woman? Why do you think we rarely see her modeled in media? What kind of woman do you want to be?

_____

_____

_____

5. What's the biggest lesson you learned from this chapter?

_____

_____

_____

_____

Chapter 22

Not So Innocent

Hey, princess . . . don't eat that apple!

Casually dating Brandon had been fun, and it sparked a new phase of dating for me. I figured out I could have the benefits of someone's attention without feeling a lot of pressure or commitment. On top of this, I recalled my dad's words about his college glory days and how a week didn't go by without several dates. Funny how I hung onto that image . . . yet, I forgot how my dad's relationships had twice ended in divorce. Well, all I knew at the time was that several guys were interested in me, and the casual dating scene would allow me to see all of them. Hey, if guys wanted to take me out to the movies or a nice dinner, why not? It didn't even matter that I had no interest in some of them. I mean, it was just casual, right? Yep, I was feeling pretty good about myself. (See any warning signs? Maybe one about how pride comes before a fall?)

So, in addition to Brandon, there were three other guys who had my attention that freshman year. One was Steven. We had reconnected my senior year after he broke up with his girlfriend. However, he was now off at a different college, and the distance between us was greater than ever. We mostly connected in the computer lab, messaging back and forth when I was supposed to be doing homework. We talked and flirted online in ways that we wouldn't have in person. I hoped that meant we were getting back together. But the flirting online gave me a false sense of intimacy, because we never once picked up the phone to really talk. Then one day I got a message I didn't like: he was back with his girlfriend. *Stink!*

The news from Steven was softened, however, by the fact that there were other guys around to occupy my time. One of those guys was a friend of Coleson's named Daniel. He was two years older than me, but he was also cute and sweet and humble and romantic! He sent flowers and notes . . . and I felt like putty around him. I was overwhelmed by the fact that this really great Christian guy would even be interested in me. And I was kind of in love with the idea of love. The problem was that Daniel would talk about his ex-girlfriend—a lot. (Hmm, sounds familiar. Didn't this happen with Coleson?) Yep, Daniel was still in love with her. In fact, he later ended up marrying her!

Now the last guy to catch my attention that year was Brent. I almost don't like to think that I ever went out with Brent, but I also don't want to leave out part of the story . . . even if it's not the best part. Brent came into the car dealership to do an audit. He was sort of good-looking, but he seemed to think he was really hot stuff and that everyone should be in awe of him. Well, I wasn't impressed. On the other hand, the other ladies in the office were. And when they discovered he wanted to ask me out, the pressure was on. "What could it hurt to just go out to dinner?" they said. Then I got a delivery of flowers. This guy was pulling out all the stops! So I caved . . . again.

Brent took me to a really nice restaurant in a really nice car. He seemed to have money, or at least flaunted it like he did. He was also older than me—I was nineteen at the time, and I thought he was in his later twenties. Well, dinner was delicious and the company was fine, so no harm done, I thought. Brent lived two hours away and was only in town for the audit, so I didn't plan to see him anymore. Yet somehow, there he was, back at the dealership, and asking me out again. With my casual dating attitude, I thought, *Why not? Why not let this guy take me out to nice places if he really wants to?* And he did . . . nice restaurants and movies and even the theater.

Then, one weekend we decided to go to an amusement park. Brent suggested that I drive up the night before and stay at his apart-ment—so that I wouldn't have to get up and drive so crazy early in the morning. I was a bit hesitant, but he had roommates, so it wouldn't be just us, and it would help with my drive. So I convinced myself it wouldn't be a big deal. Unfortunately, he did try to put the moves on me that night—and he was hoping for more than a kiss. *What had I gotten myself into?* I pretended to be really sleepy and ignored his "moves." Looking back, I think he knew I was young and naïve, and he was after my innocence.

I later found out that Brent was much older than he'd led me to believe. Talk about a wolf in sheep's clothing! He had deceived me, and I was disgusted—not just at him, but at myself. I was going out with a guy I didn't care about just for the fun and attention, and I was mak-ing very poor choices. Brent was a really strong guy, and he could have taken advantage of me if he had chosen to do so. Oh, I still thank God for protecting me from what could have been an even more awful situ-ation. I felt so stupid for thinking what I was doing was innocent. I also realized that I hadn't been listening to my Christian friends during this time. They told me later that they had been really praying for me—they knew this wasn't a good situation.

This is the part where my pride led to the fall. I had been feeling really good about myself up until this. Multiple guys had wanted to go out with me, and I liked the attention. But I had been a fool, and Brent was my big wake-up call. *Ew!* It still makes me sick to think I was so stupid and blind. But isn't that what Satan does to us—blind us to the truth? He makes us think only of our immediate pleasures and desires so that we don't see the consequences.

Satan whispers little lies in our ears to make evil seem innocent. He whispers things like:

- What can one drink really hurt? It's not like I'm getting drunk.
- So what if my boyfriend and I like to hang out alone at his house?

- I just want to see what it's like.
- One little cut won't kill me; maybe it will even help me feel better.
- Reading explicit stuff isn't like I'm actually looking at porn.
- I like TV teen dramas. They're interesting, and it's not like I'll ever do that stuff.

The truth is that Satan is out to *destroy* you! Like the witch in the story of Snow White, he offers you gleaming apples that are filled with poison. Don't take the apple! Be wary of those little things that aren't so innocent. Have people in your life who will hold you accountable—people who love the Lord. If you ever start to pull away from those people and start listening to others who say, "What will it hurt?" it's time to take a big step back and reexamine your life.

What I Learned

Satan takes little things that *seem* harmless and innocent—and uses them to push you toward danger and away from God.

Beware of false prophets who come to you in sheep's clothing but inwardly are ravaging wolves. You'll recognize them by their fruit. Are grapes gathered from thornbushes or figs from thistles? In the same way, every good tree produces good fruit, but a bad tree produces bad fruit. A good tree can't produce bad fruit; neither can a bad tree produce good fruit. Every tree that doesn't produce good fruit is cut down and thrown into the fire. So you'll recognize them by their fruit. (Matthew 7:15–20)

Girl Talk

1. What things have you seen or done that you thought were innocent, but turned out to be not-so-innocent?

_____

_____

_____

2. Why do you think people in movies seem to be having such a good time with a drink in their hand? Why does Hollywood make you laugh at things that actually go against God's teachings? What tactics like these have you seen Satan use? What is Satan out to do in your life?

_____

_____

_____

3. What are the warning signs that you might be headed down a dangerous path? How can you and your friends help protect each other?

_____

_____

_____

4. Trouble often starts with one question: *What could it hurt?* This question usually goes hand-in-hand with peer pressure. How do you stand up to peer pressure? What do you think of what Paul says in Galatians 1:10? Do you try to please God or people?

_____

_____

_____

5. What do you think about my casual dating attitude? What are your motives behind dating—or any activity you're involved in? Are your motives selfish or selfless? Are you honoring yourself or honoring God? Are these things helping you witness or helping you fit in?

_____

_____

_____

_____

Chapter 23

Letting Go

So where is the happily ever after?

Dating was a roller coaster of ups and downs. The thing about roller coasters is that if you never get off, you get sick . . . and I was. Dating seemed so pointless. There had to be more to relationships than what I was experiencing and what I had seen in the media and tabloids. At least, I hoped there was more. Where was the happily ever after? Or were fairy tales just make-believe? *Oh God, please tell me there is more to life than this empty pursuit of happiness. There must be more!*

It's amazing how God's answers can sneak up on you at unexpected times and in unexpected places. The answer to my "there must be more" plea came one night while listening to a speaker for Campus Crusade for Christ. The guy talked frankly and passionately about relationships, dating, marriage, and the Christian walk. His words gave me a lot to think about. When I examined my own relationships, I felt like I fell short. I had tried every kind of dating there was. I'd dated the cute guy, the fun guy, the bad boy, and the pastor's son. I'd tried committed dating and casual dating . . . and still no prince charming. I couldn't make a relationship last no matter how hard I tried, and I didn't know what to do anymore.

When I got back home that night, I felt hopeless. I stood in front of my bathroom mirror with my hands gripping the sink and tears streaming down my cheeks. I stared at my reflection and confessed, "I can't do this anymore. I give up. All I want is You, God! I am completely happy with just You and nobody else. In fact, I don't want anyone else. I'm stopping my search, and I will wait. Wait until you decide to bring me the one." And I let go . . .

It was a short conversation between God and myself that night; yet, it will forever be imprinted in my mind. Did I see magic fairy dust after I spoke those words? Did I feel miraculously transformed? Did I feel like I had come to a mountaintop with God? No. I felt like I had come to the end of my rope, but for the first time I was okay with letting go. I felt peace in surrendering control of my life to God and falling into His arms, trusting that He would catch me and that He was enough. For the first time, I didn't need anything else to make me happy. I was a hundred percent content . . . just me and God.

Do you know the story of Jesus and the Samaritan woman at the well? Take a couple of minutes and read John 4:1–29. God revealed a huge lesson to me in this story—and I think He'll teach you something too.

Jesus asks the Samaritan woman for a drink of water. Normally, Jews didn't hang out with or talk to Samaritans—ever. So the woman asks, "How is it that You, a Jew, ask for a drink from me, a Samaritan woman?" (v. 9). It's as if she's saying, *Who am I that Jesus would talk to me?* Have you ever thought you weren't good enough for God to love and bless you—so you just settle for whatever is in front of you, hoping it will be enough?

Look at Jesus' answer: "If you knew the gift of God, and who is saying to you, 'Give Me a drink,' you would ask Him, and He would give you living water" (v. 10). Essentially Jesus is saying, *If you knew who I was—someone who loves you unconditionally, is willing to die for you, and has all things under His control—well, you would expect so much more!* Not only was Jesus offering her (and us) eternal life in heaven and freedom from sins, but He was also offering a full life here on earth. In verse 14,

Jesus explains, "Whoever drinks from the water that I will give him will never get thirsty again—ever! In fact, the water I will give him will become a well of water springing up within him for eternal life." That means Jesus will give you a joy that bubbles up from within your spirit—a satisfaction and contentment that only comes from God.

We're all seeking to quench our thirst. The Samaritan woman was obviously looking for her happiness in guys. Jesus called her out on it too.

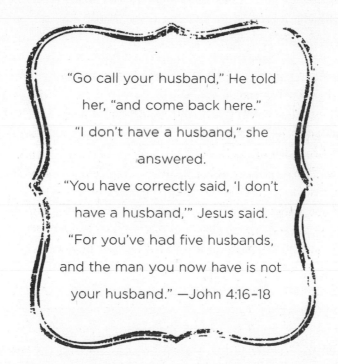

"Go call your husband," He told her, "and come back here."
"I don't have a husband," she answered.
"You have correctly said, 'I don't have a husband,'" Jesus said.
"For you've had five husbands, and the man you now have is not your husband." —John 4:16-18

Wow! The Samaritan woman was chasing after happiness in pretty much the same way the world tells us to today—and she was missing it. *Wait! Lightbulb moment!* I was missing it! *I* was the woman at the well! And maybe *you* are too!

We can't quench that deep-down desire we have with the stuff of this world—no matter how hard we try or what we turn to. For many girls, it's getting attention from guys. For others, it's the social scene, alcohol, drugs, pornography, or body image. It's whatever you keep going after to try to make yourself happy. You think if you finally get that "thing," then you'll be complete. But the truth is, when you get it, you're only satisfied for a moment, then the thirst comes back again. So you go back to the well . . . again and again and again, but you're never satisfied. That's because what you need is not physical; it's spiritual. Jesus says drink from *Me*, and you'll never be thirsty again. That's the answer!

That night at my bathroom sink was the first time I completely let go of my dating life and let God take over. And for the first time, I wasn't thirsty. I had accepted the living water Jesus offered!

Oh, and here's my favorite part of the story: "Then the woman left her water jar, went into town, and told the men, 'Come, see a man who told me everything I ever did! Could this be the Messiah?'" (vv. 28–29). Do you see it? The woman left her water jar—as if she didn't need it anymore. She knew that Jesus could quench her thirst. I too finally saw that only Jesus could quench my thirst as I left dating behind that night. It's crazy, though, because I still had no concept of the magnitude of what I'd just done or how big God really was . . . but I was about to find out.

What I Learned

You can stop the search, because what you need is right in front of you—you just may not yet realize who He really is and what He's offering.

❧

Trust in the LORD *with all your heart, and do not rely on your own understanding; think about Him in all your ways, and He will guide you on the right paths. (Proverbs 3:5–6)*

Girl Talk

1. Wow, one short talk with God completely changed my heart. It wasn't that I didn't know God before, but I hadn't given Him control of that part of my life before. Is there part of your life that you're holding

back from God? What might come from giving that part of your life to God?

_____

_____

_____

_____

2. Are you willing to let God have ultimate control in your life? What would this look like daily?

_____

_____

_____

3. Do you feel that if you aren't actively pursuing a relationship that you'll miss out? Do you think God needs your help to make it happen? What does God really want from you?

_____

_____

_____

_____

4. Have you had those moments when you feel like, *Who am I that God would even notice me?* Read Ephesians 3:16–19. What can God's love do for you?

_____

_____

_____

_____

5. God pursued me until I realized just how much He loved me and that He wanted to be my everything. He will pursue you too—just remember, my journey took a while. So when things don't go your way or you're feeling unsatisfied, ask yourself these questions: How is God pursuing me in this situation? What is He trying to teach me? Is this my chance to really trust God and grow our relationship?

_____

_____

_____

_____

Chapter 24

Like the Pieces of a Puzzle

What if God has something better for you
than you can even imagine?

Part 1

Well, it was summertime again, and I bet you can guess what I had planned—Youth Tour! But this time it was *college* tour! The program this year was called "The Witness," and it was all about Jesus. Jason and Carol Ann were going, too, so I would get to spend the summer with my two best friends. I had so much joy in my heart and was so much happier not being tied down to a guy who wasn't the one God wanted for me. I was having a blast being single, and I seemed to enjoy things even more, knowing that God had my future all under control.

One night on the tour we visited a church having revival. I was sitting next to Jason as we listened to the preacher. I can't remember what all was said, but I know Jason started feeling convicted about all of his superficial dating and relationships, and for the first time, he realized the emptiness in them. He decided to break up with his girlfriend and wait for God to show him "the one." *Crazy!* I hadn't told Jason anything about the conviction God had put on my heart about not dating until it was the right one. It was just God working in both of us. Jason slipped away soon after and made the phone call. I was so proud of him. God was growing us, and it was exciting. So, there we were . . . no boyfriends, no girlfriends, just good friends.

The tour ended with a trip to Six Flags. I love roller coasters (except the dating one), so we were all running from coaster to coaster when Jason and I spotted it—the Sky Coaster. You were strapped into a harness in a flying position and pulled to the top of a really high arch behind you. Once up there, you pulled a cord that would send you flying through the air. No one else was interested, but as always, I could count on Jason to do something adventurous with me. We paid extra to do it, and all of our friends stayed to watch. I made Jason pull the cord because I was freaking out a little. Okay, here . . . we . . . *go-o-o-o! Ahhhhhh!!!* I screamed bloody murder, but then started laughing. That was amazing!

My Sky Coaster experience felt kind of symbolic of what I had been going through. I realized that fear so often kept me where I was—on the ground with what I knew and where I felt safe, trapped in the same old way of thinking. *How could I not date or keep searching for a husband? I can't find him if I'm not looking, right?* But God was inviting me to go to all new heights with Him, to trust that He had me securely strapped in for the ride of my life. It was a scary leap of faith, but once I let God have control of everything in my life—including dating—it was like I was soaring through the air. And it was *fantastic!*

As the day at the park ended and we headed toward the front gate, Jason and I decided to stop at a caricature artist and have our picture done. Our friends all watched while the guy sketched, then suddenly they all started laughing. When the artist turned the picture around, we saw what they were laughing about. In the drawing, I was looking straight ahead and smiling, but he had drawn Jason looking down at me with a heart coming up from his head as if he were in love. I guess that summed up our relationship. Jason had always kind of liked me that way, but we both knew we were just friends and could laugh about the picture.

After the tour ended, I kept on working, going to church, going to movies with friends, hanging out, getting to know my roommates better (I'd gotten my own apartment!), and seeing family. Letting go and waiting on God had turned my summer into a very relaxing and joyous time for me. God was in the driver's seat, and I was just along for the wonderful ride.

August came and sophomore year was starting up. I didn't have a teacher like Ms. Walls again, but now my challenge was what classes I should take. I met with a guid-ance counselor who asked what I wanted to major in and then asked me if I had a five-year or ten-year plan. *Umm,* I wasn't sure what I was going to eat for lunch, much less what I was going to do with the rest of my life! It was actually kind of freaky to think about; yet, I was learning to trust that God held my future. I told the counselor, "I

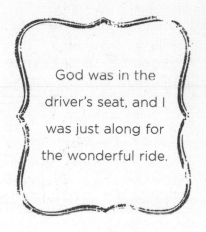

God was in the driver's seat, and I was just along for the wonderful ride.

don't know," but what I should have said was, "Well, just like the dis-ciples, I'm following Jesus. And honestly, you never know where He's going to take you." Which was—and is—so true.

Then, one day, a junior friend of ours started telling Jason, Carol Ann, and me about how much he liked his communications major. I didn't even know there was such a thing! He said it was pretty fun and not that hard. Well, long story short, we all ended up majoring in com-munications (though we did choose different minors). In a way it seemed kind of funny that we all chose that direction, but, honestly, we could apply communications to anything. And I have to admit, it was also a lot of fun sharing classes together.

I was still parking at Jason's house and walking to campus to save some time and money. Jason had gotten one of those powered stand-up scooters, so he started riding it to campus. There was just enough room for me to stand behind him if I held on tight, so I hesitantly started rid-ing with him. I say *hesitantly* because I was about 10 percent scared, but about 90 percent worried I would look like a dork! However, it did get us to campus in half the time. So, I just tucked my head behind his back and hoped no one recognized me.

That year, Carol Ann, Jason, and I decided to try ballroom dancing. It was a morning class and made for a fun way to start off the day. Jason, of course, was my usual partner. Honestly, he was the only one I felt like I danced well with. So when the instructors said to change partners, we typically ignored them.

A little later into the year, Jason and I decided we should go somewhere to try out our new dance moves. We found a restaurant with a live swing band about two hours away. *Road trip—oh yeah!* We didn't realize until we got there, though, that it was actually a really high-end restaurant. We were by far the youngest people there and could only afford an appetizer off the menu, but it was still an interesting adventure.

The drive home felt especially long after a night of dancing. I was half asleep when we got back to Jason's house where I had left my car. He got out and came around to give me a hug good-night. I reached my arms over his shoulders and laid my head in the curve of his neck. As he gave me a gentle squeeze, I thought, *We fit.* I'm not sure if I said that out loud or just to myself. I was just surprised at how perfectly we fit together— like two puzzle pieces locking into place. Funny . . .

Part 2

A few days later, I met up with Jason after classes, and we headed back to his house to get my car. Neither of us really had any plans, so we thought we'd hang out for a little bit. Out of the blue, Jason looked at me and said, "Why don't you give me a little friendly kiss?"

Okay . . . now you have to understand that Jason had been trying to get this "little friendly kiss" ever since high school. We even had kind of an ongoing joke about how the Bible says to "greet each other with a holy kiss." You also need to realize that Jason flirted with everyone, but especially me. We were the best of friends (and I guess he kind of liked me at times), and he just thought it would be interesting to kiss me. And lastly, you need to understand that Jason had the talent of driving someone absolutely crazy if he wanted to. It got to the point that I decided to give him a peck on the lips just to shut him up. I mean, we had both kissed other people before, right? So I leaned in for this quick, nonromantic kiss. But after our lips touched for just a moment, we both jumped backward, landing on opposite ends of the couch, speechless. You talk about sparks—it was like fireworks went off without any warning! When we finally faced each other again, we both said, "What was that?" I mean, it was only a small peck. It wasn't even meant to be romantic . . . and it completely blew us away!

Suddenly my mind was flooded with the events that had led up to this day. Eyes opened wide, we both said, "You're *THE ONE!*" I couldn't tell you who said it first. We both knew in that moment—it was a revelation from God. It's as if I'd had blinders on before, and now I could suddenly see everything so clearly. The pieces of the puzzle had come together in God's perfect plan, and I had found God's will for who I was going to marry! *Holy cow!*

God's revelations kept flooding our thoughts as we discussed how amazing God was in His wisdom and grace to have kept us from dating one another. We both agreed that our immaturity would have messed things up if we'd dated back in high school. I marveled at the fact that instead of superficial dating and physical temptations, God allowed Jason and me the opportunity to build on something so much more—a rock-solid friendship. I never had to play the dating game with Jason or pretend to be someone I wasn't. We'd never been anybody but ourselves when we were together. We had already accepted each other—the whole package—the good and the bad, the imperfections, annoying habits and all. Our love was genuine. What a relief that I didn't have to pretend to be perfect for some guy. I was already who I was supposed to be for the right guy—God's guy.

I finally realized the magnitude of what I had done that night in front of my bathroom mirror and of what Jason had done at the revival. Our summer of letting go was God's way of making sure that we were where we needed to be in our relationships with Him so that we could have a healthy relationship with each other. After we finally found ourselves completely content with God alone and trusted in His will for our lives, He was able to bring us together and bless our relationship. This relationship wasn't my doing; it was God's. *I had a relationship personally given to me by God!*

You know what else this meant? Since God pushed for me to find myself complete in Him first, I didn't have to lean on Jason for my self-esteem. I didn't need to use him as my security blanket or let him become my idol. Most of all Jason didn't have the pressure of filling the hole in my heart. He couldn't anyway—only God could. No, Jason didn't define me, he complemented me. He was my best friend—the guy who would live this life in love with me. He would sharpen me and encourage me in my walk with Christ, and I would do the same for him. We knew that no matter what came our way, we had that day and that moment to look back on and we could never have any doubts. How cool is that? This was better . . . better than any fairy tale ever written. *This was real! Because God is real!*

Then I started thinking . . . if God had orchestrated all this, then what else was He doing? What else did He have planned for my life that was bigger than I could imagine? I had so much joy and excitement, I needed to let other girls know that they didn't have to settle for less—that God had so much joy waiting for them if they would be patient and seek Him! I needed to tell them we really *can* have the fairy tale!

What I Learned

God is bigger than I ever knew He could be, and He has a tough, yet wonderful path to a fabulous ending for each of us. To find it, though, we must first find Him.

Now to Him who is able to do above and beyond all that we ask or think according to the power that works in us—to Him be glory in the church and in Christ Jesus to all generations, forever and ever. Amen. (Ephesians 3:20–21)

Girl Talk

1. So if God is always orchestrating things for good and for the purpose of bringing people to Him, then are you looking for His work in

your everyday life? Don't give things up to coincidence or luck; instead, look for God at work! How have you seen God this week?

_____

_____

_____

_____

2. God wants better for you than you even want for yourself. If you truly believe that, how should that affect the way you live and the way you make choices?

_____

_____

_____

3. God's ways are not our ways, and God's timing is not our timing; yet, they are both perfect. When my life doesn't quite seem to make sense or go the way I think it should, Isaiah 55:8–9 helps me. How do these verses affect your thinking?

_____

_____

_____

4. Completely trusting God with my future not only gave me tremendous peace and joy, but it also gave God a freedom to really work for something great in my life. So what if the missing piece to your life puzzle is found by seeking God's will above anything else? Would you be willing to drop everything to follow Him (Mark 1:17–18)?

_____

_____

_____

Chapter 25

A Reflection

At last . . . the shoe fits!

❧❧❧❧❧❧❧❧❧❧❧❧❧❧

I might as well have been Cinderella on the day she slipped her foot into the glass slipper and heard the words, "It fits!" Jason and I *did* fit—and everything was so much more special because of how God had built our relationship. On our walk to class the next day, we even paused with the thought, "I guess we should try holding hands?" What an odd thing to even contemplate. We both had dated, and holding hands seemed somewhat trivial; yet, this relationship was different. Our fingers interlocked and the biggest smiles came over our faces. We finally got it right. We needed a relationship founded on Christ and the rest would follow. We knew we had found the real thing!

Unfortunately, Jason and I both realized that we had cheapened and devalued those three special words . . . "I love you." In the past, we had thrown them around, just like saying "Hi" or "Bye." We had used it to mean "I'm interested in you," "I'm attracted to you," "I feel good about myself when I'm with you," or "If I say this, maybe you'll stick around." But now God was showing us what actual love looked like for the first

time. So we decided to wait to say "I love you" until the time seemed right
and there was once again real meaning behind the words.

I still remember the day it
happened. I found myself at Jason's
house with tears streaming down
my face. Honestly, it had just been
a rough day with my roommates.
I remember that Jason smiled and
asked, "Do you want me to cheer
you up?" I nodded, and he put a
CD in. As the music started playing, I realized it was my favorite
love song. Jason reached out his
hand and asked me to dance. Now,
you may think Jason and I danced
all the time, but actually we only
did fast swing dancing. We *never*

God was showing
us what actual love
looked like for the
first time.

slow danced together. So I slid my arms over his shoulders, and we
danced. As my tears ceased and he held me tight, he whispered, "I love
you." "I love you too," I said.

Okay, now tears were streaming for a different reason. Then, he
reached into his pocket as he took my hand. He slowly slipped a ring on
my finger—a promise ring. It was a promise to do this relationship God's
way, to wait until marriage to have sex, to always love me unconditionally, and to one day take me as his wife. Okay, I think he succeeded in
cheering me up!

How could this guy love me so much, and I hadn't seen it before?
Why did it take me all these years to fully accept his love? Those questions actually apply to two men in my life: Jason *and* Jesus. For as long as
I had known Jason, he was my friend, my buddy, someone to run back
to when things didn't work out well with someone else. He was my rock
and someone I could count on . . . but I never let myself fall for him. Part
of that, I know, was God's timing, but another part was that I didn't
know what real love looked like. Jason was always pursuing me, though.
He never gave up on me, and he loved me even through my stupid mistakes, my selfishness, and the times I took him for granted.

Sound familiar? Jesus was always the Rock I ran to when I needed Him most. He was my Buddy, my Friend, the One I could always count on. But I sometimes took Him for granted. Of course, I loved our relationship, but I hadn't ever let myself fall completely in love with Him. That is, until that night in front of my bathroom mirror when I finally gave Him everything. You can know Jesus and try to be His friend, but if you haven't given Him your all and decided to follow Him wherever He leads, then you haven't really experienced love at its greatest.

What a wonderful example of Christ I saw reflected in my relationship with Jason—to be pursued with such love. Jason accepted me just as I was. Honestly, I couldn't really do anything to make him love me more. He just did. And he somehow always managed to make me feel beautiful, even when I didn't feel that way. So how much more do you think God—my Creator—loves me and thinks I'm beautiful? Loves *you* and thinks you're beautiful? You don't have to earn God's love—just accept it. No strings attached.

What I Learned

Our relationships should reflect Christ, not the world.

The one who does not love does not know God,
because God is love. God's love was revealed among
us in this way: God sent His One and Only Son into the world
so that we might live through Him. (1 John 4:8–9)

Girl Talk

1. Does your current relationship reflect Christ? How so, or how not?

_____

_____

_____

2. It's hard to imagine that someone loves you unconditionally, flaws and all, but God does. Read Romans 5:8 and Ephesians 2:8–10. What does God say about His love? Read Romans 8:35–39. Can we lose God's love?

_____

_____

_____

_____

3. God created you, has a plan for you, thinks about you all the time, and is always with you. You were no mistake. Read Psalm 139:13–18. How beautiful does God think you are?

_____

_____

_____

_____

4. Have you let yourself completely fall in love with Jesus? What might that look like? Make a list of things you do when you're head-over-heels in love.

_____

_____

_____

_____

5. What truths have you found from following my search for "the one"? What did I mean by "I found the real thing"?

_____

_____

_____

_____

Chapter 26

Don't Settle

Yes, you really are worth the wait.

Now that I knew who I was going to marry, I had a whole new perspective on dating. As I looked around me, I saw couples with great relationships who kept Christ at the center. Then I also saw other relationships I recognized all too well. I saw girls who were dating just to have someone. They were running to that well of guys, trying to fill the thirst that only God can fill, only to find themselves empty again.

I watched one girl hold onto a guy just because he had been around most of her life. He was her security blanket, and it was too uncomfortable to let him go. It didn't matter that he brought her down, got her into trouble, and was only in the relationship for what he could get out of it. I realized more than anything that girls were settling . . . settling for less than what God wanted for them. The truth is you can even be with a *great guy,* but if he's not the one God has for you, then he's still the *wrong guy.* I just wanted to shake these girls and say, "Why are you settling?" Don't you know that God has an amazing love story just for you?

I couldn't figure out why these girls were settling—or even why I used to settle. That is, until one day when I was driving home from work. I was thinking about my relationship with Jason and how blessed I was, when my thoughts suddenly turned to the pain of my parents' divorce. Then I starting thinking about all the relationships that I knew were struggling. My sadness soon turned to doubts and questions: *So why should my relationship be any different? Why would mine make it when so many others haven't?* An awful, sinking fear gripped me . . . until I remembered the truth: *Because if God brought this relationship together, He can hold it together.* And the fear was gone. Whoa! Clearly Satan was trying to plant seeds of fear and doubt. And truthfully, those seeds would have taken root if I hadn't known that it was God who brought Jason and me together . . . and He would sustain us.

The driving force behind why we settle is . . . fear.

So that's it. The driving force behind why we settle is . . . fear. And it is powerful! Fear of not being good enough. Fear of not having a family. Fear of being alone. Fear of not being loved. Fear that this is as good as it gets. Fear of losing him. And then there's the fear of making the wrong choice.

Girls always ask themselves, "How will I know if *he* is the one?" Well, on our own, it is a bit of a guess and, therefore, an open door for doubt. You've got to know what it is that your relationship is going to be centered around, something that will keep you together for the long haul. You don't know how things will be in five, ten, or twenty years, or what obstacles will come your way. It can all be very overwhelming and scary. That's why I knew I needed something much bigger than me to hold a relationship together. Relationships are fallible. I'm fallible. But God isn't! If Jason and I (or any couple) would keep God, who never changes, as our focus, then we would have a steady foundation through the unpredictable years ahead. So I no longer had to fear. Why? Because there's one driving force even bigger than fear, and that is true love. The Bible says that perfect love casts out fear (1 John 4:17–18). Because I had experienced perfect love from God, I had nothing to fear.

There is no fear in love; instead, perfect love drives out fear.

—1 John 4:18

I knew I had found a truth about life: we don't have to settle! Now, I wanted to share it with the world. *(Hmm, maybe one day I could write out my love story from God for all the world to read.)* I took my opportunities to share as they came, and God soon gave me a very public one! As part of a speech class that Carol Ann and I were taking, we were given the assignment to debate a controversial topic—any topic so long as there were people on both sides to debate it. We decided to talk about waiting to have sex until you're married. Why not take the opportunity, right? There were certainly people at college with different perspectives on waiting, and two guys decided they would happily oppose our position.

I would love to say that the debate was a landslide and that everyone in the room decided to wait until marriage to have sex. Unfortunately, I don't think that was the case—though I do think God used that opportunity to plant some seeds of truth. It was really eye-opening to hear what the guys on the opposing side had to say. First, they said relationships were like buying a car—you want to see how it performs before you buy it. *Really? Okay, so who wants to have a performance-based relationship? And does that mean you get traded in when another pretty girl comes along? I don't want to be just another notch in someone's bedpost. I want to be special—special enough for someone to wait for and fully commit himself to.*

Next came the "trying different flavors of ice cream" analogy. You want to try different flavors to figure out which is your favorite, the guys said. *Okay, are you feeling sick yet? I hope I'm more than a "flavor" to my husband. What happens if his "tastes" change, and he wants to try a different flavor? Please, if you ever hear a guy compare intimacy to buying a car or picking out an ice cream—run!*

I began to realize that girls have a lot to overcome in order to find their fairy tale endings—fears, horrible "try-it-before-you-buy-it" attitudes, and also the pack of lies that the world continuously throws at us about love. Some of those biggest lies come from Hollywood. Hollywood may make movies about love, but do they really know love—true, lasting love? We see Hollywood's fairy tale weddings—the beautiful couples, the wealth, the fame—and we think, *That's what I want!* Yet, have we forgotten how those same faces pop up in tabloids, fighting through bitter divorces or custody battles, or chattering about their newest relationship? No, Hollywood's not happy, so why do we let them mold our ideas of happiness?

I met a girl once who told me flat out, "I did it Hollywood's way and got burned." She had followed the model of quick, passionate relationships she saw in the movies, romance novels, and TV shows, and it was devastating. Not only was she hurt by it, but her relationship with God was also hurt. Her disobedience drove a wedge between them. It makes sense. How can you hear God clearly when you're blatantly choosing to do things your own way (or Hollywood's way) rather than His? Our relationships aren't meant to reflect Hollywood; they're meant to reflect Christ. The good news is that once she gave her life back to God, her relationship with Him was restored. That's another amazing thing about God, by the way. Even if you've messed up, He still has a fairy tale ending for you. I knew a Christian girl who had moved in with her boyfriend and had been intimate. But then they were convicted by God and committed to not even kiss until they got married. She said it was like everything was made new. Her relationship with God was restored, and her relationship with her husband was stronger than ever before. If you've taken a wrong turn, remember that God's there to help you make a new start—to help you turn around and get back on the right path to your fairy tale ending.

I understand. I'm guilty of it too. Hollywood and the American Dream have molded me in many ways, and I'm still breaking through the wall of lies they've built. That money, a great career, fame, a huge house, and security are what we are to strive for—when instead we

Therefore, if anyone is in Christ, he is a new creation; old things have passed away, and look, new things have come.
—2 Corinthians 5:17

should be striving for God and His Kingdom, not settling for the treasures of this earth.

Quite honestly, I'm still learning how not to settle. But now I know I don't want to settle for anything short of God's best. Even if that means turning down something that seems glamorous and easy. Even if it means going against the flow. Even if what God calls me to do doesn't make sense to others—or even to myself. Just think of guys like Noah and Moses and David. They did things that people thought were crazy, but God had *big* plans for them. God will call you to do things that are bigger than you too. And it can be scary, because Satan will attack. But *trust* that God is big enough, *believe* He is working for good, and *know* that He will never leave you.

What I Learned

Seek God's best; never settle for less!

❧

There is no fear in love; instead, perfect love drives out fear, because fear involves punishment. So the one who fears has not reached perfection in love. (1 John 4:18)

Girl Talk

1. Have you ever heard those "try-it-before-you-buy-it" lies? What do you think about a performance-based relationship? What pressures does this view put on a relationship?

_____

_____

_____

_____

2. My question from the beginning has been: How do you have a lasting relationship? Can you answer that question now? What does a lasting relationship have to be founded on and why?

_____

_____

_____

_____

3. What fears are driving your decisions and maybe causing you to miss out on God's best? How can God's perfect love conquer those fears?

_____

_____

_____

_____

4. What did I mean when I said I had to break down the lies that Hollywood and the American Dream have sold me? How could money, a nice house, and fame be anything but good? Is seeking God's will for your life always the easiest, most glamorous path? What might it look like?

_____

_____

_____

_____

5. Disobedience to God's Word and direction will cause a wedge in your relationship with Him. If you haven't heard Him lately, could it be because you haven't listened to what He's already told you in His Word?

_____

_____

_____

_____

Chapter 27

The Search

There is a path that leads to your fairy tale ending,
but you have to choose to follow it.

I want you to ask yourself something: If you're searching for "the one," and all your hopes for happiness rest in what might be in the future, are you really living *now*? You see, when God is in your life and you're seeking His path for you, then you don't have to wait to find your happily in the ever after. You can find it right now!

Your story doesn't revolve around one magical moment or one magical guy. Your story is in you and in what you let God do with your life. Yes, I know that I got that eye-opening kiss when God revealed His will to me, but the magic wasn't in the kiss; it was in the journey and the revelations God taught me along the way. It's during your journey that you discover where your strength comes from. It's where you find the courage to fight for something greater—instead of settling for what is common. It's where you walk through the fire, but come out stronger and more beautiful than ever before. It's where your faith grows as you learn to let go and trust God's will rather than your own. Yes, your path will be hard and scary at times, but you can have hope because God is always at your side. But it's a choice *you* have to make. You can choose to let God lead you to an amazing ending, or you can choose to go your own way down the path that ultimately leads to destruction.

In my own journey, I had great friends like Jason and Carol Ann, I had a mom who prayed for me daily, I had my church, and I had God. If I hadn't had those pushes to keep me on the right path, I can't imagine where I would be. In every story, there is someone who pushes the main character in their search. They can either cheer them on or hold them back. They can give godly wisdom or foolish, worldly advice. Some people may selfishly guide you down the wrong path so that they have company in their troublesome lives. Some will want to harm you, while others will want only the best for you. Who is your guide? Hollywood, the media, your peers, or God? What are their motives? What do they want for you? These are things you need to know.

Sometimes we are like the little girl I saw one day at the grocery store. While she was asked to wait, she took notice of all the pretty packages within her reach. I watched as she grabbed a candy bar, but her dad quickly took it away, saying, "No, you don't need that." The little girl's face wrinkled and her arms went to her hips, "But I want it!" Then she reached for it again. It was a battle—the parent knew what was best for his child, while she knew only what she wanted. Isn't that what we do sometimes? Unfortunately, our temptations are usually bigger than candy bars. They tend to be things like sex, drugs, alcohol, pornography, lying, stealing, unhealthy food, cheap highs, gossip, and wrong relationships. They're all wrapped up in pretty packages like that candy bar, and all we have to do is reach out and grab what we want. Then God says no—and that's when we throw our fit. But God is so patient with us. In His wisdom and love, He continues to tell us that's not what we need. Though we may not always understand, He is out to protect us and save us for something better.

The little girl didn't understand that her father wanted what was best for her. Do you understand what your heavenly Father wants for you? Sometimes we look at others around us, at the movies, or at whatever else is dangled in front of us and we want it. Is it the best, though? Psalm 73 is about a man named Asaph, who looks at the world around him and is confused by how the people who oppose God and do sinful things seem to prosper and have the good life. He asks himself, "Did I purify my heart and wash my hands in innocence for nothing? For I am afflicted all day long and punished every morning" (vv. 13–14). Then, in verses 16–17, he says, "When I tried to understand all this, it seemed hopeless until I entered God's sanctuary; then I understood their destiny"—their destiny was ruin.

Like us, Asaph had wondered, *What's the point? Am I following God and living for Him for nothing?* But when he went looking for answers from God, the Lord helped him see that those people were on the path to destruction. So Asaph held on. He took the harder path. He didn't grab the temptations right in front of him; instead, he trusted in God's plan and His timing. Asaph knew God's path was the only way to true life.

In Psalm 73:21–25, Asaph finishes by saying,

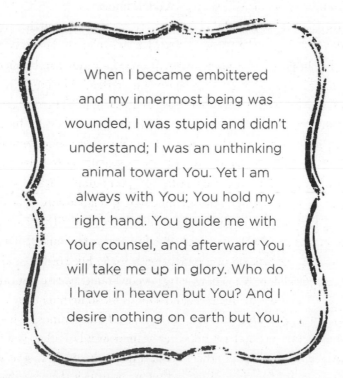

When I became embittered and my innermost being was wounded, I was stupid and didn't understand; I was an unthinking animal toward You. Yet I am always with You; You hold my right hand. You guide me with Your counsel, and afterward You will take me up in glory. Who do I have in heaven but You? And I desire nothing on earth but You.

Asaph finally saw past his own frustrations and temptations and realized what his heavenly Father offered him. I know I'm definitely like that little girl in the candy aisle. I don't always see clearly why my heavenly Father doesn't give me what I want, when I want it. I know He gives me what I need, but it's sometimes hard to wait when there are so many pretty packages in front of me. In order for me to take the harder path of waiting until marriage, of declining the popular party scene, of being ridiculed for being a different kind of girl, then I needed to know it was worth it. I needed to know if what God said in His Word was keeping me *from* something or saving me *for* something greater. Just like Asaph, I needed to know the truth about the character of God and where His path would take me. And I also needed to know Satan's characteristics and where his path led. Throughout the Bible, God reveals to us the truth about what He wants for you and what Satan wants for you. Let's take a look:

Satan wants to . . .	God wants to . . .
steal, kill, and destroy (John 10:10)	give us abundant life (John 10:10)
trick us with lies (John 8:44)	guide us with truth (John 14:6)
destroy us (1 Peter 5:8)	make us new (2 Corinthians 5:17–19)
tempt us with things of this world (Matthew 4:1–11)	give us a way out of temptation (1 Corinthians 10:13)
accuse us of our sins daily (Revelation 12:9–10)	give us grace and forgiveness daily (Lamentations 3:22–23)
put us in bondage (Luke 13:16)	set us free (Ephesians 2:1–5)
cause harm (Luke 9:42)	heal us and carry our burdens (Mark 1:34)
bring fear and doubt (Ephesians 6:12)	give power and love (2 Timothy 1:7)
offer us riches that don't last (Matthew 6:19)	offer us riches for eternity (Matthew 6:20)
take us to hell with him (Matthew 13:37–42)	prepare a place for us in heaven (John 14:2–3)
lead us on an easy path to destruction (Matthew 7:13)	lead us on the more narrow path to life (Matthew 7:13)

I point out these truths because they can easily get lost. We forget that God has given everything to pursue a relationship with us and only wants the best for us. We forget that Satan is out to tempt us and destroy us. We forget to be patient and wait for what is better. Satan's path always leads to pain and destruction, but God's path always leads to hope and salvation.

⁂

Did my search for love end like I thought it would? Well, no. I ended up on the less-traveled path. I didn't find love like in the movies—I found something so much better! I will never again doubt that God's way is best. God has proven that He wants better for me than I even want for myself. My choice to obey Him and His Word set me on the path to finding my fairy tale ending. And that path awaits you too.

What I Learned

God will guide you along the less-traveled path. It will be harder, but it's the hidden trails that always lead to the best treasures.

⁂

*Make Your ways known to me, LORD; teach me Your paths.
Guide me in Your truth and teach me, for You are the God of
my salvation; I wait for You all day long. (Psalm 25:4–5)*

Girl Talk

1. What are you waiting on to fulfill you? Has it consumed your life and become an idol you need to get rid of?

_____

_____

_____

2. You may be saying, "Are we there yet?" But nothing makes you grow more on your journey than waiting. What character traits grow out of learning to wait well? After you list some, read Isaiah 40:31.

_____

_____

_____

_____

3. Like Asaph, maybe your life seems to "stink" right now, while everyone around you appears to be living it up. How can you avoid grabbing at temptation while you're waiting?

_____

_____

_____

_____

4. What if the thing you're pitching a fit over isn't what you really need right now? Could it be that God is protecting you and saving you for something better? What does the Bible say in Matthew 6:26–34?

_____

_____

_____

_____

5. Are you willing to let God guide you on your journey (not the media, not your peers) to an all-new adventure of living for Him?

_____

_____

_____

_____

Chapter 28

Your Fairy Tale Ending

Don't you know that you are the princess?

~~~

So you may be asking yourself, what do fairy tales, princesses, princes, frogs, castles, and happily ever after have to do with God? Well, I know a girl's heart, and I know what we girls dream of. We dream of being the princess who is loved and adored. We dream of one day finding the prince, who will love us, protect us, and guard our hearts. Someone who will fight for us and go to the ends of the earth to rescue us (maybe even while riding a white horse). Someone who will lay down his life for us. And with him, your life will be made complete. With him, you'll experience true love, and there is no greater thing. That's what we dream about, isn't it? That's what we long for—we're just not sure that the fairy tale really exists. Oh, but it does . . . and you're already part of it!

Like Cinderella, maybe you've had a glimpse of the fairy tale. Maybe you once had hopes of a happily ever after, but then the clock struck midnight and it's back to reality. And just as a young girl named Ella once lost her identity in the cinders and ashes of her world, you too may not know who you really are anymore. Yet, Cinderella left behind a shoe, a trace of her true identity—and that's where the pursuit began. Just as Cinderella's prince searched for her so that he could bring her back to him, your Prince searches for you—His princess. Or do you still not see your true identity? Perhaps somewhere along the way you've forgotten it. Or perhaps the world has told you that your mistakes make you unworthy of being a princess. But the search for you has already begun. Jesus, the Prince of Peace, is pursuing you because He wants to bring you back to Him.

You see, Jesus loved you before you ever even knew Him. He accepts you for all that you are, and He wants to be with you always. He wants to protect you and guard your heart. He is ready to fight for you and rescue you. He's already laid down His life to save you. He is searching for you. And in Him, you will find true love and, yes, there is no greater thing. Jesus is the Prince you've been searching for.

That's the real fairy tale ending! *I* am a princess. *You* are a princess. That's our true identity. Our identity cannot be found in this world.

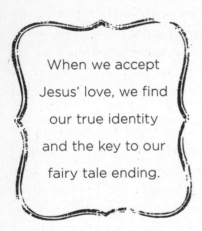

When we accept Jesus' love, we find our true identity and the key to our fairy tale ending.

The world will call us names, treat us cruelly, and try to make us feel anything but special. But through it all, don't forget this one truth: your heavenly Father is King and His Son, the Prince, is coming to take you as His bride one day. And, oh yeah—there's even a white horse (Revelation 6:1–2)! Wow, the fairy tale is true! And to think, *you* are the princess in this beautiful love story.

I did find my fairy tale ending and my happily ever after. I know, some people say it's impossible, but I say they've just been looking in all the wrong places. *So,* you might ask, *Is Jason perfect? Is your life perfect?* No, of course not. *Well then, you say, you haven't really found your happily ever after.* Oh, but Jason isn't my fairy tale ending—he's the result of it. To me, "happily ever after" isn't about finding happiness in something or someone; it's about finding a never-ending love that will never fail when we fall in love with Jesus. When we accept Jesus' love, we find our true identity and the key to our fairy tale ending, our happily ever after. In Jesus, we are made complete and right with God. In God, we find our way. We find the path that fulfills us like nothing else in this world can. Being in God's will—well, it's the "perfect fit" we've been searching for.

There's nothing like following God. It doesn't really matter whether God's will is for you to be rich or poor, to live in the United States or a third world country, to be single or married. It's just being in His will— wherever that may take you—that brings your life unexplainable joy. Some people think that "happily ever after" is a life without hardships or trials, but that's not the case. It's a difficult road to travel, but it's not one you travel alone. God will never leave you and His love will never fail. He will use your life for a bigger purpose. Whatever comes, you can take comfort in knowing that the ending will be amazing when you accept Jesus' love.

Maybe you're like me, and you've searched for love in different people, different ways, and different things, and you keep coming up empty. But all this time that you've been searching for true love, true love has been pursuing you. Jesus desires for you to be His bride, beautiful and dressed in white because He has cleansed you from your sins (Revelation 19:7–8). He is coming back to take you home to Heaven one day. The Bible describes that day as the wedding day—and what a day that will be!

Until that wedding day comes, I consider this time of waiting my "dating time" with Jesus—the time to spend getting to know Him more deeply, and to work on becoming more of the princess and bride I am meant to be. Honestly, I still have a lot to learn. I'm still learning how to better be a reflection of Him and His love, and I'm constantly learning to trust Him with my life. So I'm thankful for this time and this amazing journey I'm on—the journey that's led me to my fairy tale ending.

✿

Well, my engagement time with Jason was coming to an end. One beautiful ring, along with its promise, wrapped my finger. Another ring would soon be placed next to it, finishing the covenant. A never-ending circle, representing a never-ending love. God was right: we could truly love each other because He had first loved us (1 John 4:19). Our wedding day would be a reflection of what He had done for us. On that day, people would see a glimpse of Christ and His love for His bride.

As the bridal music started to play, I took one last deep breath, trying to take in all the excitement and anticipation. I could only hear the sound of my heart beating faster as a silence fell over the room. The doors swung open, and I stepped into the doorway. Everyone rose to their feet. My eyes quickly searched down the aisle to find the man I loved. When I spotted him, I smiled and started walking, my gaze fixed upon him. This was the day—the one God had planned for me all along. This was the day I got to marry *my* prince charming!

What I Learned

The fairy tale—the happily ever after—it all begins and ends with God.

"For I know the plans I have for you"—this is the LORD's declaration—"plans for your welfare, not for disaster, to give you a future and a hope. You will call to Me and come and pray to Me, and I will listen to you. You will seek Me and find Me when you search for Me with all your heart." (Jeremiah 29:11–13)

Girl Talk

1. Did you know that your longing for a fairy tale ending can come true (Psalm 37:4)? Maybe you've been looking for it in a guy here on earth, but do you now see how Jesus fulfills every single thing we desire our Prince to be?

_____

_____

_____

_____

2. Everyone is desperately searching to be loved, because there is no greater thing. So how does it feel to know that while you've been longing for it, Perfect Love has been pursuing you?

_____

_____

_____

_____

3. Your true identity is found in Jesus, not in your past and not in what other people say you should be. Have you lost your identity? How can you live out your true identity as a princess of the King?

_____

_____

_____

_____

4. You were created to impact God's kingdom. Jesus told His disciples to tell other people the good news about Him. What is that good news? Are you sharing it?

_____

_____

_____

_____

5. So, you're a bride of Christ. How does that change your view of your relationship—your "dating time" here on earth—with Jesus?

_____

_____

_____

_____

The En~

If you were reading a typical fairy tale story, this page would read "The End." But Jason wasn't the end of my fairy tale; he was the beginning. My wonderful journey of learning what God has planned for me is bigger than anything I ever imagined. I know there is more to come. God holds my heart, and I will follow Him anywhere. And I hope you will too.

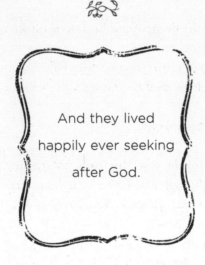

And they lived
happily ever seeking
after God.

Are You Ready for Your Fairy Tale Ending?

If you feel a desire deep in your heart to really know God for the first time and follow Him . . .

If you believe that you are a sinner (like all of us) in need of a Savior . . .

If you believe Jesus died on the cross so that your sins could be forgiven . . .

. . . then you can call on God.

Jesus said, "I am the way, the truth, and the life. No one comes to the Father except through Me" (John 14:6). Jesus is the *only* way to salvation. Read Romans 3:23, Romans 6:23, Romans 5:8, Romans 10:13, and Romans 10:9–10 for yourself.

I can tell you all about God whom I love, but He has to reveal Himself to you (Revelation 3:20). If He has, then pray and tell Him you know you have sinned. Tell Him you believe Jesus died on the cross to pay for those sins and was raised from the dead. Then ask God to forgive you of your sins. Let Him know you're ready to accept His love and live for Him. When you do this, He will give you the Holy Spirit (which is God living in you) to guide you and encourage you. Once you've made this commitment to Jesus, share it—with your family, friends, and church! Celebrate it with baptism (Matthew 28:18–20). And we at Girls Living 4 God want to encourage you and walk with you too. Please contact us at www.GirlsLiving4God.com. We are so excited you have found the greatest love there is!

Continue to hang out
with Dechari and other
Girls Living 4 God {GL4Gs}
and hear what they're learning, share, connect,
book an event for your area, and more!

Standing 4~ Faith . Purity . Light . Love

Learning to Seek God's best, because we don't want to settle 4 less! ~GL4G

What if the focus of your life wasn't about you?

THE BIG PICTURE

MAKING GOD THE MAIN FOCUS OF YOUR LIFE

GOSPEL HAYLEY & MICHAEL DiMARCO

The Big Picture is a gospel-centered book for teenagers and young adults that tells the story of the God who has always been with man and, through his Son and Spirit, always will. Best-selling authors Hayley and Michael DiMarco guide readers to be more aware of God's presence with us today and better sense His call for us to make disciples of all nations.

The gospel didn't begin in the New Testament. It was there, "In the beginning," at the genesis of everything. Across the whole of human history, God's grand narrative of love and redemption has been unfolding, a love gloriously displayed at the cross. This is the story of Jesus, and all history and Scripture point us to this good news.

Teenagers live in a world defined by pressure—and with no shortage of opinions on how they should handle it. In *The Big Picture*, teens will develop a bigger perspective of Scripture and how the story of Jesus Christ ties it all together and how He should be our main focus. Nothing brings life into focus like the gospel!

THE GOSPEL PROJECT FOR STUDENTS

B&H

Every WORD Matters™
BHPublishingGroup.com

YOU NEED COURAGE

TO LIVE FOR GOD.

TO FAITHFULLY LEAD YOUR GENERATION.

Courageous Teens is a student-focused presentation of *Courageous Living* by Michael Catt, senior pastor of Sherwood Baptist Church and executive producer of the hit film COURAGEOUS.

Catt brings fresh insight to "stories of people in the Bible who displayed great courage when it would have been easier to play it safe . . . (who) challenge me to keep moving forward. They demand that I examine my priorities and deal with anything that brings fear to my heart."

Teen readers will be inspired to resolve to live for God as they learn more about Abraham, Moses, Nehemiah, Ruth, Daniel, and many more.

Best-selling youth market author Amy Parker arranges the heart-stirring material into four categories: Courageous Faith, Courageous Leadership, Courageous Priorities, and Courageous Influence. Discussion questions are also included at the end of each chapter.

B&H
Every WORD Matters™
BHPublishingGroup.com